Hawk of Pandora

A 9/11 Missing Link

By Thomas "Hawk" Hellstrom

Hawk of Pandora: A 9/11 Missing Link

Copyright © 2010 Thomas "Hawk" Hellstrom

ISBN: 978-82-93124-00-9

Published by LTT Independent Publishing

Printed and bound in the U.S and UK

Cover design: John B Hansen
Cover Image © Author of Hawk of Pandora

Contents

Hawk of Pandora

In Memory and Honor of my Father who always showed what true courage and love was straight from his heart. I owe my mother an enormous debt of gratitude for her devoted support and being a good mother.

A special thanks to my partner, described as Paul, for his courageous dedication and covering my back in the time of need. This book is in honor of my colleagues, friends and mentors who have gone that extra mile in their attempts to help others without any recognition in return and especially to those who have placed their lives at risk and made immense sacrifices to keep this world a safer place.

This book is also dedicated to all the whistleblowers that have sacrificed enormous losses, endured the pain and suffering by exposing abuses within their environments. Never give up on your search for PEACE. God bless you.

Hawk of Pandora

Forward

Events that people experience throughout their lives, whether positive or negative, will as a fact stay embedded with them throughout the course of their life until they die. Perpetual experiences shapes and forms your individualistic personality as you go on throughout life. Perpetual experiences are your school of reality and your truth. Perpetual experiences conform to or with the choices we make regardless of right or wrong. Perpetual experiences define our frame of mind.

Perpetual experiences have and will be my school of knowledge. I think that most people can agree upon the fact that destructive behavior that contributes to conflicts, greed, hate or despair only leads to more misery. Why is it that people thrive on misery so much? Why do people excuse their aggressive and malevolent behavior on ideological beliefs and religious faiths? I have been many places across the world, cultures may be different but humans are the same. Aggressive and violent motives are the same anywhere. One thing was clear to me and that is destructive behavior does not come from any ideological belief or religious faith or politics or specific regions of the world. It's our dark sides of an imbalanced state of mind. We have turned blind and lost because of it! This book is about my experience about how and why I chose to defy common traits of evil that defined events before and after 911. This is my story about my stand against terrorism and tyranny. This is an untold missing link of 911.

Hawk of Pandora Part I; The Missing Link

"All that is necessary for the triumph of evil is for good men to do nothing." Edmund Burke

September 11, 2001, at approx. 11 am, I got a call from a friend "hey man, turn on the TV! Any channel! Two planes just struck the twin towers in New York." I immediately turned on the TV and saw a recording of one plane hitting the tower and then the next. News reporters were speechless as they witnessed the mayhem occurring in New York City. I was stunned but not surprised! I said, "Holy shit, it actually happened. They ignored the obvious signs and reports and this is what happens with indifference." I could almost say that I understood President Bush's reaction when he was notified that day in the classroom among children. The same awed, but dumbfounded reaction while reflecting back to the warnings that were obvious that an attack was looming.

Warnings purported by FBI field offices Phoenix and Minnesota were prevalent to warrant immediate investigations.[1] Warnings from many other agencies both foreign and domestic demonstrated just how top level officials lose insight beyond their own career visions. As they say "ignorance is bliss", but the ignorance and arrogance of those who chose to ignore warnings

---

[1] US v Zacarias Moussaoui Defense Exhibit 129

from so many credible sources and obstructed communication and thorough analysis, gave the terrorists freeway to operate as they pleased without interference from the authorities. This cost the lives of almost 3000 Americans and international citizens from different countries.

Almost immediately after the call from my friend, I got a call from work asking me to show up to work early. The public safety group I worked with was expected to coordinate safety efforts with law enforcement in a state of crisis.

Showing up at the office, I asked my chief "What if the suspects in my report were involved?"

He got furious and almost clinched my shirt and said, "There was no way! Forget about it and don't you ever mention it again".

He must have been really nervous! It was within eleven months, October 20, 2000, prior to that day September 11, 2001 that I showed him a report I wrote regarding the observance with several witness testimonies of a suspect wanted by Interpol. Not only did we observe the Interpol suspect walking the streets in Atlanta, but my other partner and I spoke to the suspect at a 24 hour nightclub while doing research without really knowing who he was at that particular time. I would soon find out.

Report: Positive ID's On Suspects Wanted By Interpol

Friday, October 20, 2000

From: Tom

To: Federal Bureau of Investigations

On Oct. 14, 2000 my partner and I were on the corner of Cane and Karma Street observing the parking lots and pedestrian traffic when a bearded man with sunglasses walked towards and passed us on Karma. We automatically noticed the man because of the sunglasses. It was getting dark out. We also noticed him observing us as well.

On Oct. 15, 2000 Paul and I were at a nightclub.

As I, Tom, went to order two beverages, I noticed a peculiar man wearing sunglasses standing next to me observing my presence. I looked at the man and noticed that he had East European features. This was the same exact man my partner and I observed on Karma Street. The man wore the same dark sweatshirt, jeans and the same tainted sunglasses. I asked him if he spoke Russian ("Vi gavareetye pa-rooskie?") in Russian. He responded that he didn't understand and that he was from Mexico. He then spoke to me in Russian (as if to test me!) which I did not understand and he repeated his sentence twice. Once I was served with the beverages I left the bar.

See Paul's report on disturbing and threatening statements made by this man.

Report on Suspect in Nightclub (dance club/bar) Atlanta, Georgia

Paul

10/21/00

On 10/15/00, Sunday morning, around 2:30 a.m. Tom and I were in' Nightclub'. Tom had talked to a man at the bar. The man told him he was Mexican. His features didn't seem Mexican to me. After an hour of checking the place out I went back to the bar and he was still alone in the same place. I approached the empty space next to him at the bar. I turned towards him and said, "Que onda, way?" [What's happening, man?"]

The man responded, "Nada nada. Hablo un poquito Espanol. Eres Mexicano?" [Nothing nothing. I speak a little Spanish. Are you Mexican?"]

He was a thin man in a black sweatshirt and jeans. He was wearing large, gradient-tinted sunglasses. His accent and features seemed Eastern European to me. He had a moderate tan. His beard was neatly trimmed. His nose was long and thin, bulging a little on the tip. He had brown eyes and thick semi-wavy black hair, his hair-line dipping down into his forehead. He seemed to be in his late 30's.

He seemed to be slightly inebriated. He was barely fluent in English. He said he was from Europe. Moments later he said he was from Africa. He repeated the word "Africa" several times and said he was Muslim. He said he was from Ethiopia. I said,

"Ethiopian women are very beautiful. In Atlanta there are many Ethiopians."

He said, "panocha. Panocha Buena."[cunt/pussy. Good cunt/pussy] (At this point I speculated that he had spent some time in Mexico the way he handled and spoke Spanish.)

We began talking about women and happiness. I said, "Happiness for me is finding a wife and having a family."

He scoffed, subtly shook his head and said, "Women are for sell."

I said "You don't want to settle down?"

He said, "One hundred dollar tonight I fuck woman, tomorrow she go. One hundred dollar." He smacked his hands together swinging one arm outward.

I said, "Yeah…but you never want a wife and kids?" He got a little agitated. He spent several minutes trying to convince me never to get married and that women were, "shit". He said, "You die; for forty days your wife wear (he made the motion of tying a scarf over his head). Day forty-one she (he grabbed his crotch and inhaled through his teeth making a hissing noise). Friend die for you. Women girl fuck…fuck. One hundred dollar no problem."

He gestured toward the throngs of people at the bar in sweeping motions. He said, "They no happy. You no happy. I no happy." The conversation continued. Eventually he said, "Everything in America cost money, twenty dollar, fifty dollar." He made a noise with his lips. He said "I have all the money I no happy. I have all America, I no happy." He continued talking in this vein and at one point abruptly stood up taking a step towards me. Slightly startled I rose as well. He said, "Tomorrow you dead. You, nothing. Nothing. Me, nothing. Nothing. (he made a gesture denoting the people at the bar) Nothing. My family in Bosnia-dead. My wife-dead. One hundred people my family-dead. My friend-dead." He picked up my pack of Camel cigarettes with his left hand and with his right he pointed to it and said, "my family" he then swiped it out of his left hand with his right making a sound effect with his mouth, "fffshhh". He raised the pack of cigarettes again this time pointing to the camel saying, "me, me" He pointed to the word "Turkish" on the pack and said, "Turk…" He swiped it out of his own hand again and said, "fffsh, gone." He threw the pack onto the bar. With two fingers he tapped the side of my neck for several seconds. I slightly squinted my eyes conveying my misapprehension of the meaning of his gesture. He said, "Tomorrow dead. Tomorrow you dead." He lowered his sunglasses a little and searched each of my eyes back and forth. His pupils seemed to be minutely dilating bigger and smaller. He tapped the side of his own neck and said, "Tomorrow dead. Tomorrow dead."

I said, "Yeah, but every day we say we dead but tomorrow always come." He said "No, no. Understand! You give head for me (he tapped the side of my neck). I give head for you (he tapped the side of his own neck)."

Hawk of Pandora

We sat down. He joined his thumbs together and said, "you me brothers…brothers". He patted his right hand over his heart and said, "thank you, thank you" as he touched my shoulder. He began speaking again. I couldn't understand what he was saying. By his tone and hand gestures I gathered he was talking negatively about something. At times he would gesture towards me, himself and the people around us. He kept asking, "You understand?" I nodded and at times would lean closer squinting my eyes to show non-recognition. After several minutes of this I got the feeling I should leave him alone. I rose and he nodded saying "thank you, thank you". He patted his heart again. I walked away. Throughout the whole half-hour conversation he rarely touched his drink (possibly rum or brandy) -which was full.

I am 85% positive the suspect described above is the same man posted on Interpol as Basaev Shamil (1999/14843).

Shamil Basaev and Suspect at Nightclub

'The star of a rebel shines brightest in the house where they built the stages of their performance and where audience is familiar. Outside is a whole different story.' Author of book

Apart from the open source intelligence concerning positive ID's on suspect Shamil Basaev and six other suspects from the same Interpol file, we spent a great deal of time analyzing the suspects' statements and behavior to Paul and others.[2]

Within this analysis, there are highly comparable characteristics between Shamil Basaev and the suspect at Nightclub. Many of these characteristics are extreme in nature but capture the initial mentality behind Chechen warrior culture both past and present.

Shamil Basaev's background has been long and extensive. According to information from expert sources, news articles and various online intelligence databases describe Shamil Basaev as a hard core chieftain warrior! Among his own compatriots, he is a legendary hero and is viewed as this century's reincarnation of Imam Shamil, the legendary resistance leader of the mid 1800's.[3] In fact, there is an uncanny resemblance between Shamil Basaev and his predecessor Imam

---

[2] Shamil Basaev Interpol Warrant 1999/14843

[3] As Russia was expanding into the Northern Caucasus in the 1800's, it ran into a significant stumbling block: the Islamic warrior - priest, Imam Shamil (1797 - 1871).
"Power Struggle in Checheno - Ingushetia," Ann Sheehy *Report on the USSR* RFE/RL Research Institute, 15 Nov 1991, p. 20.

Shamil. His persona indicates a sense of deep pride in the warrior traditions of his people as well as the Sufi Brotherhood. The suspect's demeanor indicated a similar pride reminiscent of proud demeanors by members of special warfare units.

© is Public Domain   Shamil Basaev   © Interpol
1800's Imam Shamil   Natalia Medvedeva Photo

The suspect's statements to Paul indicated hypothetical statements, which were very personal and deeply emotional. Paul got the impression that the suspect was trying to convince him of something but did not understand what the suspect meant.
The suspect stated that he was from Africa and then Ethiopia.

"He said he was from Europe. Moments later he said he was from Africa. He repeated the word "Africa" several times and said he was Muslim. He said he was from Ethiopia."

This indicates that he was referring to himself as a black person even though the suspect was a white male. It is common

---

[4] Jihad of Imam Shamil By Kerim Fenari; photograph ?
[5] Photo: Natalia Medvedeva, http://exhibition.ipvnews.org/photo_080.php Date: 1995 (Photo: public domain)

knowledge in Russia that Russians refer to Chechens as black people as an ethnic degradation.[7]

The suspect's statements concerning women are very similar to the mentality which Chechen Mujahideen held towards their women. Chechen crime groups are known for modern day slave trade of women for prostitution and also their cruelty towards women.[8] The suspect's statement's with Paul exemplifies this:

- "We began talking about women and happiness. I said, "Happiness for me is finding a wife and having a family." He scoffed, subtly shook his head and said, "Women are for sell."

  I said "You don't want to settle down?"

  He said, "One hundred dollar tonight I fuck woman, tomorrow she go. One hundred dollar." He smacked his hands together swinging one arm outward."

---

[6] Interpol file Shamil Basaev 1999/14843/original picture taken from Qoqaz.net

[7] Russian discrimination toward peoples from the Caucasus has been well docu mented. See: "Shamil Basayev - the Lone Wolf," *Moscow News* , No. 24 - 24, 30 Jun - 6 July 1995, p. 4.

[8] Women and Transnational Organized Crime Prepared by: Yvon Dandurand and Vivienne Chin

International Centre for Criminal Law Reform and Criminal Justice Policy. January 2000.

A very typical mindset among Chechens warriors' attitude towards women based on past history of Chechen Muslims is well characterized by Imam Shamil's mentor, Ghazi Mullah, a leader of the Chechen Muslim resistance in the early 1800's.[9]

- In 1829, Ghazi Mullah judged that his followers had absorbed enough of his message for them to begin the final stage. In a series of fiery sermons he urged the people to take up arms for the *Ghazwa*: the armed resistance:

  "A Muslim may obey the *Shari'ah*, but all his giving of *Zakat*, all his *Salat* and ablutions, all his pilgrimages to Mekka, are as nothing if a Russian eye looks upon them. Your marriages are unlawful, Your wives are whores and your children bastards, while there is one Russian left in your lands!"

During the Chechen wars, Chechen women were often raped by Russian soldiers, as they had been violated by Russians they were also regarded whores by Chechen mujahedeen and were often sold off to organized crime groups in Chechnya for this reason.[10] This is why many women in Chechnya were often renowned for fighting to their death before Russian soldiers could get their

---

[9] *Muslim Resistance to the Tsar: Shamil and the Conquest of Dagestan* Moshe Gammer, (Portland: Frank Cass, 1994).

[10] International Trafficking in Women from Central Europe and the NIS, Amy O'Neill, Office of Analysis of Terrorism, Narcotics and Crime, Bureau of Intelligence and Research, US Dept of State, Washington, D.C., December 16, 1997

hands on them. Today they are being used as suicide bombers in order to restore their honor and commitment to Allah.

The suspect's emotions fluctuated and shifted from his attitude towards women to a dying friend. The suspect's statements concerning his dying friend manifests with a picture from a web page on Shamil Basaev and Chechen resistance from an (underground?) Mujahedeen website called qoqaz.net.

- "I said, "Yeah…but you never want a wife and kids?" He got a little agitated. He spent several minutes trying to convince me never to get married and that women were, "shit". He said, "You die, for forty day your wife wear (he made the motion of tying a scarf over his head). Day forty-one she (he grabbed his crotch and inhaled through his teeth making a hissing noise). Friend die for you. Women girl fuck…fuck. One hundred dollar no problem."

A picture from Qoqaz.net depicted (resembling Shamil Basaev) a man looking over a wounded mujahedeen with two Muslim female nurses tending to his wounds. This picture coincided with Basaev's statement "Day forty-one she (he grabbed his crotch and inhaled through his teeth making a hissing noise). Friend die for

you. Women girl fuck…fuck. One hundred dollar no problem."
Picture was from Vedeno: Injured died after 40 days. [11]

The suspect's statements were also filled with thoughts of death
concerning friends, family and pre-figurative deaths of people in
general.

The suspect made several gestures throughout the course of the
thirty min. conversation. One gesture, which was repeated several
times, consisted of waving his arms around to include people in
the nearest vicinity. The contents of the conversation related to
value and loss of lives:

- The suspect gestured towards the throngs of people at the bar
  in sweeping motions. He said, "They no happy. You no happy.
  I no happy."

  Everything in America cost money, twenty dollar, fifty dollar."
  He also made a noise with his lips and then said "I have all the
  money I no happy. I have all America I know happy." Paul
  wrote that he continued in this vein and abruptly stood up and
  took a step towards Paul. The suspect stated, "Tomorrow you
  dead. You, nothing. Nothing. Me, nothing. Nothing. The
  suspect made a gesture denoting the people around the bar.
  Nothing. My family in Bosnia-dead. My wife dead. One
  hundred people my family-dead. My friend-dead."

---

[11] Picture from Qoqaz.net referring to statement from suspect "you die,
for 40 day your wife wear!"

The suspect's statements about the Camel pack and his odd ffssshhh (sound of a striking match) gesture with the reference to death. This may have indicated death by incineration or fission related to his family, his own preparation of death and the deaths of people in masses.

The suspect's strange gesture pointing to the camel on the pack and statement concerning the assertion of him being the "Turk" indicates a potential admission of his own self portrait as a reincarnation of Imam Shamil, the resistance leader of the 1800's:

- The suspect picked up Paul's pack of cigarettes with his left hand and with his right he pointed to it and said, "my family", the suspect then swiped it out of his left hand and with his right making a sound effect with his mouth, "fffshhh." The suspect raised the pack of cigarettes again this time pointing to the camel saying "me, me". The suspect pointed to the word "Turkish" on the pack and said, "Turk…" The suspect swiped it out of his own hand again and said, "fffshhh, gone." The suspect threw the pack onto the bar.

The Imam Shamil was an Avar, not a Turk, but like all the non-Turkic Muslim peoples of the North Caucasus, he has long enjoyed the status of "honorary Turk" and will no doubt continue to do so. [12]

The suspect also made a specific gesture twice with two different meanings. The gestures consisted of tapping the back of Paul's neck:

- The suspect tapped Paul's neck then stated "tomorrow dead. Tomorrow you dead."

This was a pre-figurative threat in general outlining a hypothetical intent and was not a specific or personal threat towards Paul.

These hypothetical intents suggested that the suspect also included everyone else in the vicinity. The threatening comment indicated a threat to a population and not the people within the night club itself.

The suspects' statements also indicate similarities with these verses in the Quran directly quoted on Qoqaz.net during an interview with Basaev and Khattab.[13] 8:12 *"Remember when your Lord inspired the Angels, "Verily, I am with you, so keep firm those who have believed. I will cast terror into the hearts of those who disbelieved, so strike over the necks, and smite them over all their fingers and toes."*
The suspect's statements may also indicate reference to quotes in the Quran from Qoqaz.net relating to "Day of Judgment". *"Therefore,*

---

[12] "Historical Perspective on the Conflict in Chechnia," *Low Intensity Conflict and Law Enforcement*, Robert F. Baumann, Vol 4, No. 1 (Summer 1995).

[13] Qoqaz.net Quotes of Wahhab interpretations of Quran, Interview with Chechen Mujahideen 1999

when ye meet the unbelievers in fight, smite at their necks till when you have killed and wounded many of them, then bind a bond firmly on them (take them as captives); thereafter is the time for either generosity (free them without ransom) or ransom (according to what benefits Islam): until the war lays down its burdens." [Quran 47:4]

Note: These verses above do not necessarily reflect or express the message which the Quran preaches. They are symbolically modified by the Wahhab, an Islamic belief that preaches an extreme form of Sunni ("Sufi Mysticism?") ideology or doctrine.[14] Emir Ibn al Khattab, a (former) top ranking leader within the ranks of Wahhab doctrine (sect?) and commander of mujahideen in Chechnya, was Shamil Basaev's strongest ally.[15] Both adhered to the extreme or ultra conservative Wahhab version and guidelines of the Salafist or Tawhid Shariah, which is rooted as one of the fundamental guidelines and ideological foundations of today's Wahhab belief. Emir Ibn al Khattab adopted his namesake from Prophet Mohammed's second Caliph and righteous companion. This indicates a clear distinction of belief that these particular leaders saw themselves as spiritual descendents of legendary predecessors of the past.

---

[14] Wahhabism http://en.wikipedia.org/wiki/Wahhabism

[15] Shamil Basaev and Deputy Ibn al Khattab invaded Dagestan late summer 1999, Nabi (2003)

Having said that, the extremist ideology is more or less the most powerful manipulation tool used further to recruit, indoctrinate and motivate hard core religious warriors and terrorists.

The second tapping gesture of Paul's neck indicated warrior like camaraderie in terms of 'you die for me, I will die for you:'

- *"No, no, understand! You give head for me (he tapped the side of my neck). I give head for you (he tapped the side of his own neck)".*

Cultural Warrior Mentality of Chechens

Many experts would probably agree that many tactics of today's Chechen Mujahideen units may stem from the tactics and methods used by the great Chechen resistance leader of the 1800's, Imam Shamil. Many hymns, stories and songs have been told and sung about the great Imam Shamil by Chechens of all ages. These quotes exemplify some samples of stories that are told from generation to generation which still hold as crucial elements of tradition and mentality held within the circles of Chechen culture described by Kerim Fenari in The Jihad of Imam Shamil: [16]

"But now, as the savage hordes of Tsar Boris the First pour down from the barbarian lands of the north to bring fire and the sword to the Chechens, it is worth remembering that the

---

[16] The Jihad of Imam Shamyl By Kerim Fenari p 2

Caucasus has always been the graveyard of invaders and the birthplace of Muslim heroes whose names still resound in the forests and valleys of that most romantic of all mountain lands."
"At their van rode the wild Cossacks, brutal horsemen who reproduced themselves by capturing and marrying by force the Muslim women who fell into their hands."

Imam Shamil, the resistance leader of the mid 1800's is a classic example of a Chechen warrior who exemplified a legendary status among Chechens throughout generations. Imam Shamil had for decades fought off the Russian army with inferior manpower and weapons and used unconventional tactics to his own advantage. His reputation of being a master tactician and the bravest of Chechen warriors earned him the feared respect of the Russian army itself. He became a myth in Chechen culture.[17] Shamil Basaev also earned himself the same exact reputation and legendary status in Chechnya for his bold tactics and his ability to strike back at the very heart of the Russian military with only a few hundred Mujahideen warriors at his command compared to the thousands of Russian soldiers and superior firepower.

The mindset of today's terrorists from the Islamic radical movements bares a manifestation of ancestors in mentality.

---

[17] *Muslim Resistance to the Tsar: Shamil and the Conquest of Dagestan,* Moshe Gammer, (Portland: Frank Cass, 1994).

Hawk of Pandora

This profile analyst on suicidal terrorism, Reuven Paz, explains how Islamic radicals believe that they are "spiritually connected" with predecessors of the past: [18]

"The main theme of the letter is the idea—deliberately fostered in the minds of the hijackers—that a direct line connects them to the companions (Sahabah) of the Prophet in the 7th Century. In all their preparations for the attack, and while carrying out their mission, they are to see themselves as fighting alongside their ancestors. They were instructed to tie their clothes around them "in the same way our good predecessors had done before you"; to be courageous, "as our predecessors did when they came to the battle"; to press their teeth together "as the predecessors used to do"; and to recite "other similar verses that our predecessors used to mention in the battlefield". They were instructed "not to forget to take some booty, even a cup or a glass of water." Taking booty was an important element in the norms of combat in early Islamic history." **By** Reuven Paz, ICT Academic Dir.

---

[18] Reuven Paz, ICT Academic Director Institute of Counter Terrorism

My Report to FBI Continues - Back at Nightclub.

As Paul was speaking with the man I stood across the other side of the bar monitoring this man's behavior. Paul had spoken to this man for approx. 30 minutes. While Paul was speaking to him, this man made certain gestures like pointing two fingers with his right hand down towards his neck slicing off to the right. He also pointed towards Paul and then himself and waved his hands out towards the rest of the guests in view as if he was including them in the conversation with Paul.

After Paul's discussion with this man, he told me that the man was very emotional and intense. He told me about the contents of the conversation, which made me believe that this man's persona was preoccupied with death and that this man seemed like he was possibly suicidal or prepared to die.

Considering the suspect's out of place behavior and his statements to Paul, I believed the suspects statements to be a potential pre-figurative threat.

On Oct. 18, 2000, I was browsing the Interpol wanted database, a common routine check (Researching criminal and terrorist intelligence) and ran a search on terrorist files. While browsing I noticed a familiar face among Interpol's wanted terrorists and discovered that a particular profile had an uncanny resemblance to the man we saw and met at Nightclub the previous weekend. There were three pictures of Shamil Basaev

(1999/14843) in this particular file and I showed the pictures to Paul to see if he recognized this man. He stated that it was a very close resemblance (85% positive id) of the man we saw and met at the Nightclub.

I immediately made a printout of these pictures, brought them to work, and also showed them to my partner Jeff who was with me the first time we observed this man. He looked at two of the pictures and also made a positive ID of this man.

Jeff also stated later that the man we saw at Cane and Karma had a distinguished limp.

The suspect, which three of us have positively identified according to two photo printouts from Interpol and the man on Karma Street and the Nightclub is deemed to our knowledge as the same man, Shamil Basaev (Interpol file 1999/14843).

Shamil Basaev Interpol Picture[19]

1999/14843 BASAEV SHAMIL
© INTERPOL

---

[19] Photo: Interpol file 1999/14843

Another photo (2nd picture above) from an article, "Are
Maskhadov and Basaev Planning To Go To Abkhazia "
allnews.ru of Shamil Basaev, February 2000 was a 95% Positive
match.[20]

Continued Reports on Six Other Interpol Suspect

Monday, October 23, 2000, I, Tom passed on pictures of
Interpol suspect to Nightclub security.

Sunday, November 5, 2000, I delivered another copy of
pictures and report to Nightclub security staff.

Monday, November 6, 2000, at approx. 2040 hrs., I received a
call on my cell phone by 'Nightclub' security notifying me that
several of the staff members have positively identified a peculiar
man, which matches the same description of the Interpol suspect.
Security officer stated "a guy with the same description as the
pictures has been coming around regularly. He comes in and sits
at the bar, orders a glass of rum, sits there for 20-30 minutes and
leaves, barely touching his drink".

Tuesday, November 7, 2000 at approx. 1945 hrs., Nightclub
manager leaves message on my cell phone stating, "hello, my
name is Chuck, I work for Nightclub, Atlanta. We have an
information sheet that was given to us about positive ID on

---

[20] Photo: Are Maskhadov and Basaev Planning To Go To Abkhazia,
allnews.ru, http://lenta.ru/english/2000/05/17/basaev/

suspect wanted by Interpol and we have recognized this individual as being in the club on regular basis and we are looking to get better pictures of Shamil Basaev so that we can make copies and pass it out to our bartenders and managers."

Friday, November 9, at approx. 0200 I returned to Nightclub and talked to Chuck after I obtained a more recent photo of Shamil Basaev. At Nightclub, Chuck informed me that several staff members had recognized a man, which fits a very close description to the suspect wanted by Interpol. He also stated that this man seemed to prefer a particular female bartender. Chuck stated that this bartender recognized this same man because of his odd behavior and that this man gave her the creeps. Chuck also made an out of the blue statement saying that he knew of Russian criminals coming to Nightclub on a frequent basis after I said that I had my hands full with a few projects.

That Friday morning I met Paul and showed him the recent picture of Shamil Basaev. After seeing the new picture Paul's ID was 95% positive of the resemblance that the man we met at Nightclub was Shamil Basaev, the same man wanted by Interpol. Sunday, November 19, at approx. 0230 Tom returned to Nightclub. While accompanied by a female friend, I noticed five other suspects who matched a very close description of five fugitives wanted by Interpol from the same Interpol file on Shamil Basaev.

Amsadov Zaourbek   Movsaev Abousoupyan   Iousoupo Rizvan

© Copyright INTERPOL

© Copyright INTERPOL

© Copyright INTERPOL

Ismailov Rouslanbek   Movsaev Tourpal [21]

© Copyright INTERPOL

© Copyright INTERPOL

Movsaev Tourpal (95% positive ID from the new sketch)

There were two other individuals accompanied by these five suspects. I overheard one of the two unknown suspects having a conversation with a girl (unknown) by the bar on the second floor. According to the conversation the girl was trying to guess where the man was from. The man then stated to her that he was from

---

[21] Interpol warrant Shamil Basaev file 1999/14843 (warrant has since been altered) Sketches were created by author of Movsaev Tourpal based on Interpol picture and suspect at nightclub, however due to the likeness between sketch and the Interpol picture it cannot be published.

the Russian Federation. He also stated (hinted) that he was from part of a region north of the Caspian Sea. He did not specify the name of the region. The lady nodded to him as if agreeing with him, but could not guess the region. The suspect then introduced her to his friends, the other five suspects. The suspects first spoke Russian between each other and then introduced themselves to the girl. The second unknown suspect had gone downstairs.

I went to the bar downstairs and I noticed that the second of the unidentified suspects was standing at the first floor bar. I went to the space next to the suspect by the bar and ordered a coke and a beer. His demeanor appeared to be calm and settled while he was viewing others around the bar. I pulled out a picture of Shamil Basaev and noticed the suspect glancing over and looking at the picture. I could sense a nervous tension about him as he began fidgeting with his pack of cigarettes. He looked at me for a brief moment and then looked away as I turned my head to look at him. I could tell that he started losing his cool because the more he looked at the picture of Shamil Basaev the more uneasy he got. Stood at the bar next to the suspect for approx. 40 minutes. From his behavior and his continuous peeking (sometimes staring) at the picture of Shamil I could tell that he knew of this man. The man left the bar and went up-stairs. Moments later the second suspect came down again and proceeded to go outside followed by one of the other suspects (Ismailov Rouslanbek?) a minute later.

© INTERPOL
Aslan Edisoultanov

Thursday, November 23 at approx. 0100, I attempted to reach manager Chuck at Nightclub to gather written testimonies without any success. I had been told that manager Chuck had been transferred to day shift. I proceeded to check around to gather further information concerning the suspects when unidentified suspect (#2) sat upstairs at the bar speaking to another person (an entertainer at Nightclub). At that time I had a copy of Interpol file 14773 of Movsaev Tourpal. Suspect (#2) was also identical to suspect Aslan Edisoultanov, (based on the sketch with long black hair and 3rd picture). As I observed the suspect he also noticed my presence. He stood up and went over to the phone and made a phone call. After the phone call the suspect went over to the person he had talked to and left the premises through the back

---

[22] Interpol file 14773 of Movsaev Tourpal/Picture Aslan Edisoultanov (Sketch of this suspect with long black hair was created by author based on Interpol picture and suspect at nightclub. Due to permission restrictions sketch cannot be displayed).

(patio door). I attempted to get a direction of travel but suspect had disappeared out of view. I sat next to the person (the entertainer) and struck up a chat with him and asked where his friend came from. Apparently the suspect told this person that he was from Cyprus, Greece. During the conversation the entertainer appeared to be suspicious concerning my presence.

Saturday, December 16 approx. 0430, at nightclub, suspects Movsaev Tourpal and Amsadov Zaourbek kept me under observation as I was accompanied by a friend (a former U.S intelligence officer). Suspect Movsaev stood across the bar as suspect Zaourbek stood approx. 8ft behind me off to my left. It was apparent from Movsaev's behavior and gestures that he was pointing me out to suspect Zaourbek. As I turned my head, Zaourbek seemed to acknowledge or confirm Movsaev's facial gesture. At that point I notified my friend that it was time to leave due to some potential danger. My friend observed my behavior and acknowledged the two suspects that I pointed out (she had no knowledge of the situation in progress). I then escorted my friend out to her car and she left. I proceeded back inside. The suspects were gone. This was the last time I saw any of the suspects.

I submitted the rest of my report which I faxed directly to Joint Counter Terrorism Task Force Special Agent, Federal Bureau of Investigations, Atlanta Ga. On Dec. 30 after my first report was submitted on Oct. 20, 2000. See Fax next page.

```
HP LASERJET 3150                                      SEND CONFIRMATION REPORT FOR
PRINTER/FAX/COPIER/SCANNER                            ████ ██████  ATL
                                                     404█ ███████
                                                     DEC-30-00   7:16PM
```

404

JOB	START TIME	USAGE	PHONE NUMBER/ADDRESS	TYPE	PAGES	MODE	STATUS
598	12/30 7:05PM	11'23"	404████████	SEND............	15/15	96	COMPLETED....................

TOTAL   11'23"   PAGES SENT: 15   PAGES PRINTED: 0

Fax

To: ████████ (Federal Bureau of Investigations)
From: ████

Subject: Positive ID's On Potential Interpol Suspect's

████

I work for ███ █████ and passed previous reports to him to pass on to the appropriate authorities. Since then there has been further activities which should be brought to your attention. I am sending you further reports on what I have of information concerning the circumstances. I spoke to Dr. ████████ and he suggested that I send this directly to you.

████████████

Pg. 4/4 ████ - ████

It was apparent that no follow-up of any kind had been conducted after my first report was submitted due to the fact that the security staff and manager from Nightclub followed up with me concerning the staff's respective concern of the first suspect even after I had advised both security staff and manager to contact FBI and Interpol directly. I even gave them phone numbers they could call. It was naturally flattering to receive the trust of handling the situation but still fundamentally risky handling that kind of situation when it called for a whole group of the best counter terrorism experts to deal with the caliber of these specific terrorists.

February 2001; between one and two months later, two of the 9/11 hijackers, Mohammed Atta and Marwan al-Shehhi show up in Decatur, Lawrenceville and Norcross, Georgia for flight training. Mohammed Atta had resided in areas around Atlanta for a short period traveling back and forth between Georgia and Florida.

"Returning to the United States later that month, on January 25, 2001, Atta and al-Shehhi moved temporarily to Norcross, Georgia, where Atta visited the Advanced Aviation Flight Training School in Lawrenceville, Georgia. The two performed flight checks at the Advanced Aviation on January 31, and February 6, 2001. It is believed that Atta and al-Shehhi remained in the Atlanta, Georgia, area through February and March, 2001. It is during this time period that a crop duster pilot in Belle Glade,

Florida, identified Atta as having inquired about the purchase and operation of crop dusters."[23]

As described in U.S. v Zacarias Moussaoui from testimonies related to Mohammed Atta and Marwan al-Shehhi's movements and activities relevant to 911: [24]

"Between on or about February 1, 2001, and on or about February 15, 2001, Mohammed Atta (#11) and Marwan al-Shehhi (#175) took a flight check ride around Decatur, Georgia.

In or about February 2001, Mohammed Atta (#11) and Marwan al-Shehhi (#175) attended a health club in Decatur, Georgia. "

There were several important links tying the Hamburg cell leader Mohammed Atta to Moussaoui and the Chechens. A key contact person, according to the indictment against Zacarias Moussaoui, Ramzi Bin al-Shibh (Binalshibh) traveled to London in December of 2000 with the intent to support Moussaoui on

---

[23] STATEMENT FOR THE RECORD, FBI DIRECTOR ROBERT S. MUELLER III, JOINT INTELLIGENCE COMMITTEE INQUIRY INTRODUCTORY REMARKS before United States Senate Select Committee on Intelligence Sept. 26, 2002.
[24] United States of America V Zacarias Moussaoui; THE UNITED STATES DISTRICT COURT FOR THE EASTERN DISTRICT OF VIRGINIA ALEXANDRIA DIVISION, DECEMBER 2001 TERM - AT ALEXANDRIA INDICTMENT

behalf of the Al Qaida/Chechen Liaisons in London.[25] Ramsi Bin al Shibh had expressed strong wishes to fight in Chechnya under Khattab. He had provided material and financial support for the 911 hijackers who either fought for or intended to fight in Chechnya including Zacarias Moussaoui.

The testimony at the Hamburg trial of Mounir Motassadeq, another Moroccan charged with helping the Hamburg cell and September 11 hijackers Mohammed Atta and Marwan al-Shehhi, revealed Motassadeq as an apparent contact for the Chechen cause.[26] "The young men, who were said to be "obsessed with Jihad" and "cheerfully" sang songs about martyrdom, "always talked about Kosovo, Afghanistan, and Chechnya."[27]

So why the silence with Mohammed Atta's and Marwan al-Shehhi's short stay in Atlanta! Why keep Senator of Georgia Max Cleland in the dark about the redacted parts of the 911 commission report? Senator Max Cleland resigned from the 911 commission in protest accusing the commission for stonewalling information, which they obviously did. Why transfer the FBI agent I was in contact with in the middle of an investigation and shortly after Atta shows up in Atlanta? The exact same obstructions as the FBI offices in Minnesota and Phoenix

---

[25] "There are no witnesses who report that Moussaoui and Binalshibh actually met in London, but Moussaoui's subsequent travel to Afghanistan implies that he received instructions from Binalshibh. They both resided at the same dorm in London. See ibid. Summary of Penttbom, p. 86., The 911 Commission Report
[26] Ibid
[27] Ibid

experienced by transferring agents in the middle of counter terrorist investigations! Makes you wonder whose side the big bosses in Washington are on?

The signs were there before our eyes yet people chose to do nothing in fear for their own selfish needs. Perhaps it is pride that allows us to make so many stupid decisions? Is it our greed that turns us blind to what's in front of us? How can we look into the mirror while forsaking so many people with blind contempt for justice?

From the republic of Georgia to the state of Georgia was a paradox of similar characteristics of corruption, organized crime and terrorism seemed to transcend neglect to hide the dark sides of our human nature.

This is our indifference, ignorance and arrogance which we create smokescreens contributing to our own failures that forge consequences at the expense of the innocent.

The Georgian Smokescreen

"As we know, there are known knowns. There are things we know we know. We also know there are known unknowns. That is to say we know there are some things we do not know. But there are also unknown unknowns, the ones we don't know we don't know."
-Donald Rumsfeld 2/2/02 Pentagon ('Brilliant'speech about knowing what they don't know!).

For Shamil Basaev and Ibn al Khattab the northern territories of the Republic of Georgia represented numerous favorable advantages.

The ruggedness of the mountains and gorges from the plains allowed for easy hit and run tactics and concealable supply routes. Unlike other Russians, Chechens and other Caucasians were naturally adapted to deal with the rough nature that surrounded the Caucasus. For the Chechens the landscape was their friend. The rough terrain was their backyard.

From the Pankisi gorge to Abkhazia Shamil had many places he could call safe havens from both the Russians and Georgians. As long as he was a respected and feared militia leader and these regions remained outlaw lands, he was in his right place.

The Republic of Georgia has had a multitude of issues to deal with claiming independence from the former Soviet Union. Bordering the Caucasian republics of Russia to the north, Dagestan to the east and Armenia, Azerbaijan and Turkey to the south has represented a number of challenges for Georgia in their efforts to change into a country of democracy. Georgia's primary motive for their pro democratic position was the growing issues of turmoil against Russia. Naturally, Georgia would become an obedient ally with the west given the many advantages of the western owned Baku oil pipeline stretching from Baku, Azerbaijan through Tbilisi, Georgia and ending in Ceyhan, Turkey. The west obviously had many interests and advantages by supporting Georgia and even the various Russian opposition clans, separatists and militant groups to the north on the Russian border.[28]

The west, especially the Bush Cheney regime of neoconservatives, was more preoccupied with picking a fight with Russia than committing to the evasive war on terrorism in the Caucasus region.

The volatile challenges represented by high degrees of corruption and organized crime combined with groups of separatists and terrorists, especially from the Caucasus have evolved in lawless conditions and regions. Consistent phases of conflict and growing extremism in Chechnya, also known as the Republic of Ichkeria, has been a continuous impetus of instability and conflict in the region. While Chechens have fought the Russians for several centuries from the 1800's to 2006 with on and off separatist wars,

---

[28] The Chechens' American friends John Laughland guardian.co.uk, Wednesday 8 September 2004 23.59 BST

Georgia has subsequently been involved as a result of proxy regions where clans and ethnic conflicts have been at odds with each other.[29]

The three primary proxy regions within Georgian borders sustainably supported by Russians are Abkhazia, Adjaria and South Ossetia breaking away from Georgia. There is also an abundance of ethnic clans caught between two opposing countries generating conflicts against either side and facilitating hotbeds for organized crime and terrorism.[30]

During phases of existential turmoil many of these different ethnic clans, breakaway regions, republics and countries involved have fluttered back and forth from side to side, from one alliance to the oppositional facilitating multitudes of corrupt, political and religious goals.

One can easily argue that the leaders of these regions and republics consistently involved in conflicts resemble a notion of multiple personalities changing alliances from week to week like a schizophrenic play script purporting "you is my bests friend in the whole world. I love you!" A week later "You is my enemy. I kill you, Infidel!"

Shamil Basaev and Ibn al Khattab defined the mujahedeen of the Caucuses in modern times. Apart from Osama bin Laden,

---

[29] Lawless regions in Georgia, Murphy (2004).

[30] Trouble in the North Caucasus, Kulikov, General Anatoliy, Fort Leavenworth, Kan.: Foreign Military Studies Office. Originally published in *Military Review*, July–August 1999.

these two were the extremist inspirations to follow for everyone who wanted to fight Russia or the West.

When Chechnya claimed independence from Russia in November 1991, after having defended Yeltsin during the Russian coup d'état of August 91, Basaev was back home in Chechnya backing Chechen leader Dzhokhar Dudayev for independence. Boris Yeltsin and his administration panicked when Dudayev announced independence and sent troops to Chechnya's border. This became the starting point of Basaev's 15 year career as an insurgent and terrorist.

Around the end of 91 and beginning of 92, Shamil Basaev and a group of his men travel to Afghanistan and Pakistan for training at Bin Laden's camps.[31] It was at these camps that Basaev became acquainted with Ibn Al Khattab, Osama bin Laden's lieutenant. Shamil Basaev, the name sake of the great Imam Shamil of the 1800's, was literally the Russians and Georgians worst nightmare of the region starting his Chechen mujahideen notoriety fighting for Abkhazia in the war against Georgia with the infamous Abkhaz Battalion in 92 to 93.[32] Then Basaev was working under Russian support against the Georgians for independence of Abkhazia and South Ossetia. Russian military intelligence (GRU)

---

[31] CRS Report for Congress; Received through the CRS Web Order Code RS20411
December 7, 1999 Afghanistan: Connections to Islamic Movements in Central and South Asia and Southern Russia Kenneth Katzman Specialist in Middle Eastern Affairs, Foreign Affairs, Defense, and Trade.

Col Anton Surikov and Ruslan Saidov, who assisted the Abkhaz
defense minister Sultan Sosnialev, was apparently Basaev's
curators and handlers on behalf of the GRU.[33] Surikov and Saidov
established reputations as the architects of local conflict in the
Caucasus and Central Asia.

Boris Kagarlitsky wrote an article, "Who blew up Russia" in
the Novaya Gazeta alleged that Shamil Basaev trained and
operated as a GRU agent conducting ('Active Measures')
sabotage and various covert operations common to terrorist
activities such as airplane hijackings, bombings and
kidnappings.[34] During the Abkhaz war, Shamil Basaev hijacked a
Turkish passenger plane and demanded safe haven for Chechens
exiled to Turkey.[35] Boris Kagarlitsky also alleged that Basaev was
under GRU instructions (Surikov and Saidov) for his role together
with his brother Shirvani in the Russian apartment building
bombings, also known as Russia's 911 with the help of FSB who
were identified red-handed placing some of the bombs.
The combination of training as GRU and at various al Qaida
camps in Afghanistan and Pakistan gave Basaev an edge that

---

[32] "Storm in Moscow": A Plan of the Yeltsin "Family" to Destabilize Russia
John B. Dunlop The Hoover Institution October 8, 2004 p42
[33] "Blowing up Russia" Aleksander Litvinenko and Feltshinski 2006 p

[34] Pro-Chechen rebels have carried out hijackings and hostage takings in
Turkey, including an April 2001 siege at an Istanbul hotel in which 120 people
were held captive for 12 hours before rebels surrendered and released the
hostages unharmed. See "Chechens in Theater Raid Linked to Turkish
Foundations" (2002).
[35] Chechen Parliamentary speaker: Basaev was GRU officer The Jamestown
Foundation, September 8, 2006

clearly benefitted his abilities as a feared terrorist leader. He always managed to stay a step ahead of the Russians and his adversaries.

Boris Kagarlitsky, Director of Institute of Globalization Studies and Social Movements (IPROG), and IPROG associates Anton Surikov, Vladimir Filin and Ruslan Saidov had intimate knowledge of Basaev's involvement with the GRU. Anton Surikov has stated openly that he knew Basaev in articles written for IPROG and Forum.msk.ru. Boris Kagarlitsky has interviewed Anton Surikov and others regarding Basaev's training and operations for GRU.

Anton Surikov, based on public email correspondence with Oleg Grechenevsky, confirmed his position with IPROG and in fact was instrumental in Kagarlitsky's appointment as director of IPROG in 2002.[36]

"After Mr. Kagarlitsky has been a director, I have agreed on a voluntary basis to become a staff member of the institute, and then introduced Mr Kagarlitsky Ponomarov with the Lord, and Kondaurova Belkovskim. In doing so, my stay in IPROG were formal. Up until that before the spring of last year, I do not know any names of officers IPROG, except the names of Lords Kagarlitsky and Ponomarev.

---

[36] Email between Anton Surikov and Oleg Grechenevsky 09/17/05
http://www.mail-archive.com/cia-drugs@yahoogroups.com/msg01967.html
original source from Cf. *Argumenty i Facty*, 9/15/99,
http://www.aif.ru/oldsite/986/art010.html.

I inform you that make it clear that my participation in the appointment of Mr. Kagarlitsky [as] IPROG director in summer 2002 and further cooperation with him in the institution until the autumn of last year did not mean that in January 2000 he wrote his article to my order, and under my dictation." Email between Surikov and Grechenevsky

There have been substantial allegations that Boris Kagarlitsky was a partner in a shadowy company called Far West Ltd. Ukrainian intelligence (GUR) Gen Vladimir Filin, Former GRU col. Anton Surikov, Chechen intelligence Ruslan Saidov, and Lithuanian Intelligence and former Lithuanian Defense Minister Audrius Butkevichius were partners in Far West Ltd which have allegedly been involved in arms and narcotics trafficking. Vladimir Filin confirmed in an interview with Pravda that Far West was cofounded by a U.S. company (KBR/Halliburton). [37] Butkevichius has himself acknowledged partnership with Far West Ltd.[38]

Audrius Butkevichius, former Lithuanian defense minister, was a seemingly very odd addition to Far West Ltd considering his passive aggressive approach to defense in Lithuania. Butkevichius's partnership in Far West was typically due to his connections to western intelligence. He would be an important asset to insure 'green lights' acquisitions and deals of arms from US and Britain through Lithuania to Georgia or even separatists in

---

[37] Ibid
[38] http://www.pravda.info/news/2695.html
Анатолий Баранов и Антон Суриков вошли в состав руководства агентств а « FarWestLtd » - 2005.05.03.

the Caucasus. His influence with billionaire oligarch Badri
Patarkatsishvili in Georgia was also an important element as he
sustained a strategic intelligence role as an advisor. Badri
Patarkatsishvili, born and raised out of a Jewish family of
intellectuals, earned his fortunes with his business partner
Berezovsky through Russia's kleptocracy during the fall of the
Soviet Union and after.[39]

During the time of Soviet Union's break up and Lithuania sought
its own independence, Lithuanian intelligence had an established
partnership with U.S and British intelligence especially with their
significant help in the defection of Vasily Mitrokhin through
Lithuania. Butkevichius himself confirmed following an article by
Vilnius newspaper Lietuvos Zinios about Lithuanian
intelligence's role in Mitrokhin's transfer to MI5.[40] Vasily
Mitrokhin was a high ranking KGB officer that defected to the
U.S. through British and European intelligence. Butkevichius
served as Lithuania's Defense Minister setting up his strategic
non violent national defense system. Butkevichius has had ardent
views against Russia. This obviously made him a popular ally in
Washington among Bush and Cheney's arms industry regime and
even among the Democrats despite being a convicted felon in

---

[39] *Obituary: Badri Patarkatsishvili*, Tom Parfitt, *The Guardian*, London, 02-15-2008

[40] Lithuanian intelligence agencies helped KGB's Mitrokhin to escape to Great Britain- *Lietuvos zinios Vilnius*- Eurasian Secret Services Daily Review 07.10.2007.

Lithuania and other allegations of criminal involvement. His positions in politics in Lithuania or Georgia and eventually being a partner with arms dealers who are all partners in the company Far West Ltd naturally played a significant role in his convictions. On the other hand Butkevichius was considered a prominent leader with the potential to lead and defend Lithuania by non violent means which made him very appealing to European countries and U.S., also made him a dangerous adversary to Russia. Butkevichius was convicted of corruption charges by receiving a $15,000 bribe by a Lithuanian oil company that sought to evade a lawsuit against the firm.[41] The weight behind the convictions of Butkevichius is definitely debatable due to his alliances and foes but also the sloppy processes of his conviction in Lithuania possibly leading to bias and false criminal claims. It happens all the time in Eastern Europe.

Butkevichius's future obviously took a turn when he allegedly bartered bribes from the oil firm and then turned to arms dealing associates in c/o Halliburton and co. while he served as advisor for oppositions in regional governments. Butkevichius was engaged in numerous campaigns against Russia to insure that neighboring countries would not fall into Russia's control. During his role as defense minister he defended Lithuania from threats of

---

[41] Annual report 1999, Lithuania International Helsinki Federation of Human Rights.

Russian incursion in 1991 without any major conflict.[42] Between
sponsorship from Boris Berezovsky and the Bush administration,
Butkevichius was one of (late) Badri Patarkatsishvili's (former
presidential candidate of the republic of Georgia) most important
support medium with the west during the Georgian "Revolution
of the Roses."[43] Badri at the time supported upcoming president
Saakashvili against the highly corrupt Shevardnadze in 2003 to
2004. Butkevichius did play a role as an architect of non violent
resistance with the way democratic processes sustained a role in
Georgia without major violent clashes that usually occurs during
power shifts in the region. This despite major corruption within
the Georgian government is a seemingly impressive achievement!
In essence of rationality, it is difficult to see how a man like
Audrius Butkevichius, a partner of Far West, could be directly
involved with mass scale drug networks and have close partners
associated to terrorist networks considering his history of non
violent revolutions. Then again many politicians have turned
blind eyes to their social networks' criminal engagements and in
Butkevichius's positions adaption to highly corrupt environments
is merely about survival. Nevertheless the consistent quagmires of
corrupt associations in the Caucasus sustains devil's advocacy no
matter which side they turn to. Butkevichius's warmongering

---

[42] SOVIET TURMOIL; Lithuania's New Defense Minister: Young Man With a
Nonviolent Strategy By STEPHEN KINZER, Published: Wednesday,
September 4, 1991

[43] Yasenev's Memo http://left.ru/burtsev/ops/yasenev_en.phtml

associates or business partners sustain representations as advocates for either side of 'evil' Diasporas in spite of their professions of supporting democratic processes. The substance of their agendas seems more likely about the power of their positions to get them where they want to go than ideological or political loyalty. All of us who support freedom certainly agrees with the need to prevent tyrant ideologies and it's corrupt leaders from gaining hold of this world but sponsoring one ideology with corrupt or criminal tyrants on one side to fight another is neither acceptable nor is it achievable. Sponsoring criminals or terrorists on one side that produce the same tyrant results only exceeds the latter. Washington's Diasporas, 'ultimate supporters of freedom and democracy' as usual would turn a blind eye to individuals with previous convictions and associated to people who support terrorism as long as it favors their agendas, foreign policies and most important commercial assets. The Bush administration had placed Iran Contra convicted felons such as Elliot Abrams and John Poindexter, to name a few, in very important and powerful positions within their own administration displaying a role model over a leadership of convicts.

- Elliot Abrams; (convicted for withholding evidence and obstruction of Justice; pardoned by George Bush sr.) was appointed the Special Assistant to the President and Senior Director on the National Security Council.[44]

- Fmr. Admiral John Poindexter: Convicted in Iran-Contra, found guilty of multiple felony counts for conspiracy, obstruction of justice, lying to Congress, defrauding the government, and the alteration and destruction of evidence, convictions reversed; Appointed as Director of the Information Awareness Office.[45]

Placing a convicted felon in control of development of global surveillance systems that would be instrumental with Bush and Cheney's worldwide surveillance program? How scary is it to think of a convicted felon in partnership with elements of organized crime (Bank of Commerce and Credit international (BCCI) or also known as Bank of Crooks and Criminals International) networks given the authority and power to develop and even use technology to snoop into private lives of anyone on this planet? This is why so many are against domestic surveillance programs because people with a history of corruption are placed into these positions of power of controlling surveillance programs that would be used to cover up their crimes and used against those who are genuine in combating crime, corruption and terrorism.

---

[44] "Personnel Announcement", The White House. http://georgewbush-whitehouse.archives.gov/news/releases/2005/02/20050202-10.html.

Their agenda for the Caucasus and Central Asia was to do anything to secure commercial interests and oppose Russia even if it meant supporting (behind the curtain) criminal enterprises or terrorists. Both Russian and U.S administrations are consequently guilty of sponsoring organized crime and terrorism to achieve their commercial and political goals. Washington provided Butkevichius and Surikov with the support they needed apparently through KBR/Halliburton and Diligence. This is obviously why Butkevichius and Surikov attended special training at the King's College, London Center for Defense Studies in England (at the same time).[46] Butkevichius has been a visiting scholar with the Albert Einstein Institute since mid 92 when he thanked the Institute for their supportive role in Baltic States independence.[47] In 1995, he was invited to spend three months for civilian based defense (CBD) studies in the Baltic's. Civilian based defense is a non-violent alternative against internal and external threats by civilian masses. This was the obvious tactic used in the Revolution of the Roses in Georgia and the Orange revolution in Ukraine backed by Albert Einstein Institute where several CIA associates teach.

Among others that were also alleged partners in the Caucasus were Khoz Noukhaev, a former leader of the Chechen organized criminal community Obshina. Khoz Noukhaev also served as

---

[45] Sutherland, John. "No more Mr Scrupulous Guy". The Guardian
http://www.guardian.co.uk/Archive/Article/0,4273,4358017,00.html.

[46] Anton Surikov, *Crime in Russia*, p38-39

member on the board of American Caucasian Chamber of
Commerce weaving substantial support from the US despite his
background as leader of Obshina and tied to associates of Al
Qaida like Basaev and Khattab.[48] Ruslan Saidov is a close partner
with Khoz Noukhaev and together set up the Chechen separatist
intelligence base in Turkey known as "Istanbul Bureau".[49]

Cheney's infamous quote about using methods of the "dark side"
certainly bares truthful manifestations to the actual "dark"
associates and business partners of Halliburton and his Neocon
patrons who have a long history of associates to organized crime
(arms dealers) and terrorism.

"A lot of what needs to be done here will have to be done quietly,
without any discussion, using sources and methods that are
available to our intelligence agencies," Cheney told Americans
just after 9/11. He warned the public that the government would
have to operate on the "dark side."[50]

Plausibility of Cheney's assertions would explain the advantages
of Neocons affiliations to Basaev and Khattab through
Noukhaev's influence in the Caucasus and Baku, Azerbaijan,

---

[47] Albert Einstein Institute
[48] "Caucasian diamond traffic" (Moscow, 2005),
http://www.civilresearch.org/pdf/7.pdf: "In spring 1997 Adnan Khashoggi
introduced Hozh-Ahmed Nukhaev to James Baker."
[49] Investigative research and profile by Burtsev.ru
[50] PBS, Frontline; The Dark Side

Surikov's influence of Sukhumi and Saidov's influence of port of Novorossiysk.[51]

By gaining secured trafficking routes from the golden crescent through Iran to Turkey or Uzbekistan, Kazakhstan, Caspian Sea through the Caucasus to the black sea coast of Abkhazia, Russian port Novorossiysk and further on to Odessa or Crimea, Ukraine or Turkey, major contraband shipments can flow freely with the protections of controlling organized crime groups and corrupt government officials through Khoz Noukhaev, Anton Surikov and Ruslan Saidov's influences in these regions.[52] All three have strong affiliations to Turkey and Ukraine. Anton Surikov's Turkish name is Aka Mansour Nathoev and related by cousin to a General of the Turkish intelligence.[53] Their partners Vladimir Illyich Filin and Alexei Aleksandrovich Likhvintsev, both former Ukrainian generals that were forced out for political partisanship activities during Ukraine's Orange revolution.[54] Filin has also been implicated with arranging the sales of Ukrainian cruise missiles to Iran. Ruslan Saidov is a highly influential partner and

---

[51] Burtzev.ru

[52] "Abkhaz smugglers deliver the drugs by truck to Port Sukhumi on the Black Sea. From there, the drugs are carried by Turkish ships to the port of Famagusta in Northern Cyprus where local drug dealers take over. On the return routes, the ships, truck and helicopters carry arms and munitions acquired by Turkish intelligence for Basaev's forces." CHECHNYA The *Mujahedin* Factor by Yossef Bodansky

[53] The above collaborates with Yossef Bodansky's descriptions. Yasenev gives descriptive profile details based on information from IPROG and Forum.msk.ru which Surikov and Saidov are members of http://left.ru/burtsev/ops/yasenev_en.phtml

[54] Ibid

considered an important figure in Chechen and Turkish Wahhab networks. He is also a military advisor to the Minister of Defense, Republic of Uzbekistan. On the other hand Saidov is associated to Hizb ut Tahrir and Islamic Movement of Uzbekistan (IMU) through old associates from his days attending high school in the Fergana Valley. Saidov has passports from Russia, Turkey and Uzbekistan.[55] He is also an IPROG associate with Anton Surikov.

With Richard Perle, Douglas Feith, Michael Ledeen and other Neocons, there is always a familiar pattern that has nothing to do with national security, diplomatic relations or peace by their expanded memberships in various "peace or freedom" oriented think tanks or committees like American Turkish Council, American Committee for Peace in Chechnya, AIPAC, U.S Committee for a Free Lebanon and etc. War mongering from side to side clearly defines their political motives with Machiavellian savvy. Richard Perle (of Jewish descent from New York) and Douglas Feith, zealous supporters of Israel say they are adamant supporters against terrorism and Al Qaida, the Saudis, extreme Islamic doctrines like the Wahhab doctrine and pragmatic supporters of military objectives against Syria and Iran. Yet, we find case after case and reports after reports from the old days of the cold war, Iran Contra scandal and BCCI to Plame gate to Sibel Edmonds evident and yet urgent testimony about Perle, Feith and the rest of the Neocon "good fellows" activities are

---

[55] Ibid

overwhelmingly associated by either business or political bed fellows with criminal figures and sponsors of terrorism like;

- Adnan Khashoggi, the famous Saudi Iran Contra arms dealer and BCCI associate which has a long list of associations with terrorist groups from FARC in Columbia to Al Qaida in Afghanistan. Adnan Khashoggi's interests in Chechnya also allowed Chechen and Al Qaida connected terrorist Shamil Basaev and other top alleged crooked figures to meet at his residence in southern France. Adnan Khashoggi was also closely associated to Khoz Akhmed Noukhaev and Ibn Al Khattab.[56] Adnan Khashoggi was invited as a business partner by Richard Perle in Trireme Partners LP.[57] Trireme Partners was a company that provided goods and services to Homeland Security and DoJ in the U.S.

- Boris Berezovsky, Russian oligarch, tycoon and financial supporter of the Chechen terrorists has strong ties to various Russian organized crime figures and numerous leaders of the Chechen Mujahideen. Berezovsky allegedly financed Basaev and Khattab's invasion of Dagestan in 1999. Berezovsky even admitted giving two million dollars to Basaev claiming it was meant to restore a factory. Israelis imposed a blockade on Gaza following economic sanctions preventing food and

---

[56] Pictures of Adnan Khashoggi and Khoz Ahmed Noukhaev together at a meeting Caucasian diamond traffic Part 2
http://www.civilresearch.org/pdf/7.pdf: Moscow June 2005.
[57] "LUNCH WITH THE CHAIRMAN; Why was Richard Perle meeting with Adnan Khashoggi?" by Seymour M. Hersh Issue of 2003-03-17.

supplies from reaching Palestinian civilians claiming that the supply shipments were providing Hamas with arms but when Berezovsky, a Russian (Jewish) émigré (with an Israeli citizenship) gives two million dollars directly to a terrorist leader (at the time was vice-Prime Minister of Chechnya but none the less a terrorist and allied with Ibn al Khattab, an Al Qaida lieutenant) in 97'- who in 95' was directly responsible for the massacre of over a hundred civilians (including women and children) at a hospital in Budenovsk and later in 95' threatened to turn Moscow into an eternal desert by nuclear annihilation– there was no economic blockade, no arrest warrant (with the exception of Dutch, French and Swiss authorities) and not even a single protest from Israel, Europe or the U.S against him. Most charity organizations (especially the leaders) that were caught supporting Al Qaida, Hamas and even the Chechens were indicted and blacklisted with their accounts frozen and rightfully so. However, instead of indicting Berezovsky, Israel protected him due to his Israeli citizenship, Britain provided political asylum under their protection and he was openly invited as an investor into a Bush family business not to mention other business ties with ATC members. Berezovsky's claim of an innocent business transaction or donation to restore a 'cement factory' was clearly accepted despite the fact that Berezovsky also admitted he knew that the money could be used for 'other purposes' i.e terrorism given Basaev's terrorist acts and close alliance to Ibn al Khattab and added to his interview with New York Times that "It was not my function to control how he (Basaev) spent the money."[58] He became responsible as soon as he handed over the money to them. Berezovsky had especially a close relationship to Khoz Noukhaev and the criminal community Obshina, according to Paul Klebnikov who was murdered after writing books of sensitive details about them. This was obviously not an important fact when President Bush's younger brother, Neil Bush, acquired Berezovsky as an investor for his "educational" software venture capital firm Ignite! Learning.[59] How many U.S and allied soldiers have died from Al Qaida allied mujahideen sent to Afghanistan and Iraq by Basaev and Khattab? Where was the respect, the Bush administration, members and family showed these soldiers and agents when Neil Bush brought a terrorism financer into the family business? Where was Cheney with his typical rhetoric about supporters of terrorism?

- Khoz Akhmed Noukhaev, high ranking leader in the Chechen Mujahideen, leader of Chechen organized crime community "Obshina" had associations to both Adnan Khashoggi and Boris Berezovsky. As a high value asset

---

[58] Russian Says Kremlin Faked 'Terror Attacks' February 1, 2002, N.Y Times
[59] http://www.baltictimes.com/news/articles/13659/ Berezovsky, Neil Bush, Latvian businessmen meet Sep 23, 2005

Noukhaev- considered missing or dead- had influences from Caucasus to Azerbaijan to Kazakhstan dealing closely to the consortium in control of the Baku oil and gas pipelines. Halliburton and several neoconservative affiliated companies had considerable interests in the Tyumen pipeline also in the Caucasus.[60]/[61] Apart from his position as leader of Obshina, Noukhaev developed the Caucasus Common Market and served as chair member for American Caucasus Chamber of Commerce in order to attract western investments into the region. Noukhaev has met with several top officials from the US on several occasions. Adnan Khashoggi introduced James Baker to Noukhaev as early as 1997. Khashoggi had substantial investments with the Caucasus Common Market.[62]

To clarify what the organization of "Obshina" is: Much like the Obshak (pooled criminal resources) that insures divisional, financial and legal cover, the "Obshina" is like the U.N. for the Chechen criminal community represented by the heads of major Chechen organized crime groups or even separatist groups involved with criminal activities. Any form of insurances,

---

[60] www.halliburton.com/ps/default.aspx?navid=1225&pageid=2517 -
[61] "Cheney Led Halliburton To Feast at Federal Trough" Center for Public Integrity (CPI) at www.public-i.org.
[62] "Separatism, Islam and Oil," . Cf. "The tendencies of interregional and international integration in North Caucasia," Caucasian Knot, eng.kavkaz.memo.ru/reginfotext/engreginfo/id/560578.html.

financial settlements, agreements or disputes between is handled by the "Obshina" as a committee with each member of the major Chechen or Caucasus crime groups. Both Khoz Noukhaev and Boris Berezovsky were regarded as "Chairmen" of the Obshina providing higher council and support from their political allies in the Duma (Russian Parliament).

The latter associations are just the tip of the iceberg.

Former GRU and Chechen intelligence officer Ruslan Saidov, having tight relations with all these elements, was in unique positions to provide opportunistic support accommodating clients like the Neocons and the Russian side with political and financial interests in war mongering and profiteering. For them it's simply pure business!

Like their Neocon partners Anton Surikov, Ruslan Saidov and their partners are central to the war mongering behind most of the conflicts in the Caucasus. Their primary loyalty sustains to the profits and power they make from their take of sponsoring arms and alleged narcotics trafficking in the region whether it be representing Russians on one hand and the Turks or the Neocons on the other. Like the Neocons the end always justifies their means. Like their Neocon partners, war and chaos supplies their means. Shamil Basaev was the perfect asset with the audacity to carry out media attractive displays of spectacular acts of terrorism like Beslan School Massacre, Russia's 911 apartment building bombings, Budenovsk hospital and the Moscow theatre siege. For either side these spectacular terrorist acts served as perfect

smokescreens for political and financial interests and agendas.
Yes, they are that cold blooded!

In June, 1995, Basaev gained his first phase into Chechen
legend by conducting missions and terrorized Russians in their
own backyard in what became known as the famous Budenovsk
siege.[63]
Basaev had hidden men into coffins that were meant for dead
Russian soldiers and passed through the last checkpoint into
Budenovsk where they were stopped and escorted to the Militia
headquarters unaware of the rebels hidden in the coffins.[64] His
men then attacked the militia headquarters before ending up
taking over 1500 hostages including over 100 children, many
women and elderly at the local hospital.[65] Basaev had demanded
an end to the first Chechen war and removal of all military
occupation of Russian forces in Chechnya. Russian forces at the
orders of the Russian government made several attempts to
engage Basaev and over 100 of his men by force. The raids
resulted in reckless and disastrous consequences causing the
deaths of at least 160 hostages including many of the women and

---

[63] "ASSAULT AT HIGH NOON" By John Kohan/Moscow; Dean
Fischer/Washington and Yuri Zarakhovich/Moscow Monday, Jun. 26, 1995
Time

[64] Basayev has given numerous interviews describing the Budennovsk raid from
his perspective. For example, see Foreign Broadcast Information
Service: FBIS - SOV - 95 - 116, FBIS - SOV - 95 - 139 and FBIS - SOV - 95 -
142.
[65] Ibid

children.[66] After successful negotiations, Basaev released most of the hostages. Basaev escaped by negotiated agreement and shielded by over 100 of remaining hostages with almost all of his men intact without any real problems back to Chechnya. Basaev even insured that eleven of his men that died were transported back to Chechnya in a freezer truck.[67] The remaining hostages were released. This gained respect by many of his countrymen and followers worldwide.

Following the Budenovsk siege, it seemed that Dudayev and Shamil Basaev were not quite done giving Russians ulcers. In November 1995, Shamil Basaev and his men apparently secured a metallic box with cesium hiding it in Ismailovsky Park in Moscow.[68] Moscow would have had good reason to be concerned because around the same time London's Sunday Times reported, cited by leaked Russian documents, of an incident with missing nuclear materials, including Cesium-137, Strontium-90 and supposedly weapons grade plutonium-239 and uranium-235 from a Radon factory at Tolstoy-Yurt in Chechnya.[69] The terrifying

---

[66] Otto Latsis, "Zestokost porozhdaet tol'ko zestokost" Brutality breeds nothing but brutality, Izvestiya, 20 June 95, pp1-2

[67]" See: Stepan Kiselev, "Hostages of the Kremlin. The Tragic Events in Buden novsk are Changing the Political Landscape of Russia,"
Moskovskiye novosti, 18 - 25 June 95, p. 5, as translated in FBIS - SOV - 95 - 141 - S, 24 July 1995.

[68] Richard Sakwa, ed (2005). "Western views of the Chechen Conflict".
Chechnya: From Past to Future. Anthem Press. pp. 235. ISBN 978 1 84331 165 2.

[69] "Nuclear materials missing at radon factory" London Sunday Times 1995/ RFE/RL Newsline.

thought of Shamil's previous training in sabotage from the GRU and his fellow Sukhumi friend and curator Col Anton Surikov who was an expert on nuclear proliferation including small atomic demolitions munitions (SADM) also known as small portable nuclear devices and "suitcase nukes" made this combination a worst nightmare. GRU's sabotage division was alleged to have been responsible for training and distribution of these devices.[70] It was also alleged that these units were responsible for distributing SADM's around the world including several locations in the U.S. One of these alleged locations was in Minnesota where Zacarias Moussaoui had been arrested. However, plausible deniability of the existence of these suitcase nukes is still a mystery. Anton Surikov's father was also one of the designers of the Russian ICBM (Inter Continental Ballistic Missiles) named Viktor Surikov.[71]

Russia, since the fall of the Soviet Union had experienced an overwhelming problem with renegades in their military. Many had gone over to conducting mafia activities and became prominent members of Russian organized crime groups.

It is unclear as to where Shamil's men obtained the cesium-137 but since the hospital in Budenovsk had technology which used cesium it is possible he got it from there. Cesium is very common

---

[70] Stanislav Lunev. *Through the Eyes of the Enemy: The Autobiography of Stanislav Lunev*, Regnery Publishing, Inc., 1998. ISBN 0-89526-390-4

and used in X-ray equipment in most hospitals and industries around the world.

Basaev then alerted Moscow with a threat that he would turn Moscow into a nuclear wasteland.

- The Threat of Nuclear Diversion Statement for the Record by John Deutch, Director of Central Intelligence to the Permanent Subcommittee on Investigations of the Senate Committee on Government Affairs 20 March 1996.[72]

"Examples of non-fissionable radioactive materials seen in press reports are cesium-137, strontium-90, and cobalt-60. These cannot be used in nuclear weapons, but could be used to contaminate water supplies, business centers, government facilities, or transportation networks. Although it is unlikely they would cause significant numbers of casualties, they could cause physical disruption, interruption of economic activity, post-incident clean-up, and psychological trauma to a workforce and to a populace. Non-state actors already have attempted to use radioactive materials in recent operations. For example:

- In November 1995, a Chechen insurgent leader threatened to turn Moscow into an "eternal desert" with radioactive waste, according to press reports. The Chechens directed a Russian

---

[71] Modernization Of Strategic Nuclear Weapons In Russia: The Emerging New Posture by Nikolai Sokov Monterey Institute for International Studies May 1998

[72] The Threat of Nuclear Diversion Statement for the Record by John Deutch, Director of Central Intelligence to the Permanent Subcommittee on Investigations of the Senate Committee on Government Affairs 20 March 1996.

news agency to a small amount of cesium-137-a highly
radioactive material that can be used both for medical and
industrial purposes-in a shielded container in a Moscow park
which the Chechens claimed to have placed. Government
spokesmen told the press that the material was not a threat,
and would have to have been dispersed by explosives to be
dangerous. According to Department of Defense assessments,
there was only a very small quantity of cesium-137 in the
container. If it had been dispersed with a bomb, an area of the
park could have been contaminated with low levels of
radiation. This could have caused disruption to the populace,
but would have posed a minimal health hazard for anyone
outside the immediate blast area."

After the first Chechen Russian war of 94 to 96 Basaev
became a national hero despite his failed attempt to become
president of the Republic of Ichkeria (Chechnya).
Nevertheless, according to case transcripts of many of the
terrorists involved in 9/11, they had attempted to join the fight in
Chechnya. It seemed as if every Islamic terrorist across the
Mideast and Asian hemisphere wanted to fight alongside Basaev
and Khattab. Many of these volunteers found haven being trained
for the Chechen cause in the Pankisi Gorge in Georgia.
According to an article written by Peter Baker of the Washington
Post "in 1999, at least 100 Al Qaeda fighters joined hundreds of

Chechens in the Pankisi Gorge on the Georgian side of the Chechen – Georgian border."[73]

In October 2002 fifteen Arab fighters in the Pankisi Gorge were captured by U.S. trained Georgian Special Forces and immediately extradited them to the U.S. Among them was the Egyptian, Saif al-Masry, a high ranking member of Al Qaida. Masry was an officer of the "Chechen branch" of the Chicago, Illinois based Benevolence International Foundation (BIF). BIF was one of the major organizations that collected charity proceeds and converted the proceeds to support al Qaida, the Chechen mujahideen and other conflict regions sustained by extremist groups.[74]

In October of 2000, press reports and various open source intelligence databases speculated whether Shamil Basaev were supposed to have been in the Pankisi gorge in the republic of Georgia, but other statements by both Georgian government and a group hunting Shamil Basaev insisted they were not in the republic of Georgia.

On November 7, 2000, the Russian ministry requested the apprehension and extradition of Shamil Basaev, Ibn al Khattab and Ruslan Gelaev and sixty-four others from Georgian territory.

---

[73] Peter Baker, "15 Tied to Al Qaeda Turned over to the U.S.," *Washington Post,* October 22, 2002, p. A17

[74] Ibid

Georgians denied their presence in Georgia and responded that they would be apprehended and extradited to the Russians.[75] For the Georgians; they would have liked nothing better than hand over Shamil Basaev to the Russians knowing that Basaev was a fervent supporter of Abkhazians and Ossetians against Georgia. Shamil Basaev was just as much of a concern to Georgians.

January 5, 2001, a Georgian militant group, "White Legion," commander expressed intentions to hunt down and confront Shamil Basaev who was believed to be "somewhere" on the Black Sea coast of Abkhazia.[76] Shamil Basaev was supposed to have been in north regions of Georgia from October to December. As described in my report was witnessed up close and personal by at least a dozen witnesses in Atlanta, Georgia due to match identifications from the Interpol warrants.

During that time, Atlanta's administration and law enforcement departments were plagued with a "culture of corruption."[77] Mayor Bill Campbell had been indicted and sentenced for corruption charges.[78] APD officers were also charged and one sentenced in the Kaplan/Gambino indictments.[79] Many other corruption cases also came to light involving law enforcement officers working as

---

[75] "Russia calls on Georgia to handover Chechen field commanders," Eurasia.org/Georgia Daily Digest
[76] Is Shamil Basaev in Georgia? RFE/RL Newsline Jan. 5 2001
[77] Prosecutors Say Corruption in Atlanta Police Dept Is Widespread By SHAILA DEWAN and BRENDA GOODMAN Published: April 27, 2007
[78] Ibid
[79] Atlanta police officers indicted Kaplan Gambino case Atlanta Journal Constitution June 6, 2001

security for night clubs and stripper bars owned by organized crime and other involvements to gang related crimes and even contract killings.[80] It seemed overwhelming. Atlanta had also been rated one of the highest murder and cop killing capitols in the U.S. The situation so raw that a police chief got wacked outside his home![81]

"Dec, 2000, newly elected DeKalb County Sheriff Brown was shot and killed outside of his home. Investigators described the shooting as an assassination style hit. Before being sworn in, Sheriff Brown had warned he would clean up corruption in the sheriff's Department. His incumbent, Dorsey, was already under investigation for allegedly using "on duty officers" for his private security company."

Atlanta's issues with corruption represented numerous problems when conducting counter terrorist investigations. Corruption has always been a counterweight for any progressive investigations by honest and legit law enforcement personnel and it always will be. When these Chechens and later 911 hijackers were in Atlanta 11 to 8 months prior, any investigative interest in these suspects were blinded by self preservation and fear by risking exposure of the corrupt activities that existed. There already was heightened awareness to corruption in Atlanta, and those involved in earning

---

[80] FORMER ATLANTA POLICE OFFICER DAVID FREEMAN SENTENCED TO PRISON IN "DIABLOS" STREET GANG CASE August 08, 2005 www.usdoj.gov/usao/gang/diablos.htm
[81] National News Briefs; Sheriff-Elect in Georgia Fatally Shot in Ambush New York Times December 17, 2000

shady extra income didn't need any more negative media exposure.

There were also Russian/Israeli organized crime activities in Atlanta.[82] As some sources from one of the night clubs (not B-Nightclub) had stated, there were Russians apparently bringing briefcases handcuffed in plain sight of law enforcement officers working as security in uniform for this club. Russian organized crime straight from East European countries did not represent a powerful presence in Atlanta compared to other organized crime groups such as Italian/American, Latino/Mexican, and Israeli/Mideast and Asian OC groups. However Russian OC groups have often shared credit or name with the Israeli OC given the greater presence of ROC groups in Israel. Atlanta's appetite for the sex industry with its many strip clubs and massage parlors sustained a market for eastern European and Asian women who often are trafficked through Israel. Israel is and has been a major hub for trafficking women from Asia and Eastern Europe to the sex industry elsewhere.[83]

"Sin city" as Atlanta is known for via its liberal sex clubs is also a major hub for narcotics trafficking. Atlanta has been rated as a High Intensity Drug Trafficking Area (HIDTA) "designated

---

[82] The Growing Threat of International Organized Crime...Hearing Before The Subcommittee On Crime Of The Committee On The Judiciary House Of Representatives One Hundred Fourth Congress
Second Session January 25, 1996 U.S. GOVERNMENT PRINTING OFFICE WASHINGTON:1996

by the Director of ONDCP, "in consultation with the Attorney General, the Secretary of the Treasury, the Secretary of Homeland Security, heads of the National Drug Control Program agencies, and the Governor of each applicable State," under the authority of Public Law 109-469, the "Office of National Drug Control Policy Reauthorization Act of 2006," ("the ONDCP Act")."[84] Much of the narcotics coming in through traffic routes from Mexico. According to Drug Enforcement Administration, several metric tons of cocaine are trafficked through Atlanta as the southeast hub by collaborating Latin American and Mexican drug cartels.[85] Mexican drug cartels have sustained a major presence in Atlanta along with the explosive influx of Latino immigrants and illegal aliens that have found prosperity in the growing metropolitan city. Chechen Obshina has throughout the years increased its cocaine trafficking activities from FARC and OC groups from Mexico to Central and South America. GRU has also had numerous assets or sleepers in Mexico since the 50's and 60's.[86]

Just from listening to quite a few of the many good officers in APD and other law enforcement dept's indicated clear signs of

---

[83] The Body Sellers: Hundreds of Thousands of Illegal Immigrants in Overseas Pipeline, Says State Department." Committee for a Safe Society. (2000, July).
[84] High Intensity Drug Trafficking Area (HIDTA) program http://en.wikipedia.org/wiki/HIDTA
[85] MEXICO'S DRUG CARTEL MOVES TO U.S: Atlanta a hub for East Coast Violence is following, but to a lesser extent By Jeremy Schwartz Cox International Correspondent Published on: 08/01/08
[86] The Sword and the Shield: The Mitrokhin Archive and the Secret History of the *KGB* by Christopher M. Andrew and Vasili Mitrokhin (Paperback - 8 Aug 2000)

frustrations at the time of many issues and problems with law enforcement in Atlanta.

The true story of New York police officer Frank Serpico is only one in many case scenarios where law enforcement officers are pressured to go "dirty" or face consequences of persecution like Serpico did. The pressures can be so severe that police are known to have high rates of suicide in areas plagued by corruption- just as described earlier from Atlanta. Many don't seem to think it's worth the bother of being a straight cop because there is so much at stake and too much peer pressure. The ones that are straight sometimes fold up and turn blind eyes because the demands they have to deal with are too immense.

Regardless of the policies any law enforcement organization has on discussing outside the box, honest law enforcement personnel will always have the need to vent frustrations especially if they are caught in peer pressure situations of corrupt circumstances within their own departments! The pressures can be so extreme that venting can be a matter of sanity or even life or death.

Take into consideration the case of the Chechens involved and how they got there, where international and local corruption and organized crime certainly played a prominent role. From the statements by the suspect at the Nightclub being Mexican, African, Turkish and Eastern European could have described his travel route which is the same trafficking routes used by organized crime groups, arms and human traffickers from the

Caucasus. The Chechen organized crime community, "Obshina," uses supply routes usually from Black sea port in Abkhazia to Crimea or Odessa, Ukraine or Turkey, Balkans, Italy and Africa to Latin American countries often in collaboration with KLA for arms or cocaine with Revolutionary Armed Forces of Columbia, also known as FARC.[87]

In 2004, there was quite a stir about a group of Chechens tracking their way across the border from Mexico to Arizona.[88] A claim by an intelligence report (not mine) alleged that a group of over 20 Chechens had entered the US from Mexico over the border from Arizona. Sparked by concerns of materials found among Chechen mercenaries in Iraq about targeting schools and institutions in the US and the Beslan school massacre west of Chechnya fresh in everyone's memory, it is not surprising that a report like that would spark some attention. That report also kicked in memories of the suspects in my reports and was an eerie déjà vu. Considering that the suspect in my report had mentioned he was Mexican and that my partner had asserted by the suspects Spanish skills that he had spent time in Mexico or at least entered the U.S. through Mexico. Initially that cross border report was refuted by intelligence as a false claim. Following the cross border report, Cheney had temper tantrums trying to convince

---

[87] Professor Bruce M. Bagley, *Globalization and Transnational Organized Crime: The Russian Mafia in Latin America and the Caribbean*
[88] "Chechen terrorists probed" Washington Post, October 13, 2004

with conviction that terrorists would use a nuclear weapon inside the U.S. while debating against John Kerry.[89]

Several other 'incidents' of nuclear terrorist threats that would lead to the Chechen group's purpose in the U.S. or perhaps misleading fear factors by Bush and Cheney's cabal of intelligence 'cherry pickers';

According to Graham Allison in his book Nuclear Terrorism October 2001, U.S. intelligence regarded new intelligence from an asset codenamed "Dragon Fire" concerning a missing 10 kilo ton nuclear weapon (SADM) in New York.[90] A dozen six man Nuclear Emergency Support Teams (NEST) were dispatched to Manhattan to run radiological sweeps over the whole island using specially equipped helicopters, unmarked vehicles and personnel on foot with concealed detection equipment. NEST teams came up empty and the threat was deemed to be a 'false alarm'.

The Bush administration regarded the possibilities of Al Qaida using a nuclear weapon in the U.S as a genuine plausibility. There is no doubt that the possibility is true. According to CIA director George Tenet in his book "At the Center of the Storm," soon after 911, Tenet and two other WMD terrorism high ranking experts were ordered by the president to fly to Pakistan on a fact finding mission regarding whether Al Qaida had capabilities of

---

[89] "Cheney, Invoking the Specter of a Nuclear Attack, Questions Kerry's Strength" by Randal C. Archibold, NY Times, October 20, 2004

[90] Allison, Graham. Nuclear Terrorism: The Ultimate Preventable Catastrophe. New York: Times Books, 2004

developing a nuclear bomb for use inside the U.S. Prior to 911 the CIA had received intelligence from assets of friendly intelligence sources in the region that Bin Laden had met with two Pakistani nuclear scientists, associated to the AQ Khan network, at Bin Laden's compound.[91] The two scientists later confessed that Bin Laden had access to or was in possession of radiological material through Islamic Movement of Uzbekistan (IMU) and sought to build a nuclear weapon or a dirty bomb. The son of one of the scientists declared that they had no intention of helping Bin Laden build a bomb. One of the scientists had previously expressed extremist views in his own book published in 87' called Doomsday and Life After Death: The Ultimate Faith of the Universe, giving a frightening description of nuclear doomsday on behalf Jihad.[92] In reality, from all of the investigations into black market proliferation networks with rogue scientists such as the AQ Khan network to terrorists willing to use nuclear materials with concrete efforts to build nuclear bombs or attempts to obtain readily available backpack or suitcase nukes (SADM's) from Russian stockpiles, there was an abundance of consistent intelligence to suggest the realistic nightmare of a terrorist cell using a nuclear weapon. With my reports regarding the Chechens, their own history with the nuclear incident at Ismailovsky Park in Moscow and the Russian nuclear engineer, the realities of nuclear

---

[91] "2 Nuclear Experts Briefed Bin Laden, Pakistanis Say" Washington Post, December 12, 2001

[92] At The Center Of The Storm (New York: Harper Collins, 2007)

terrorist attack inside the United States of America became as real and extreme as it could get.

The alleged missing nuclear weapon from the "Dragon Fire" claim that was missing from Russian stockpiles was never confirmed. U.S. intelligence at first considered it to be genuine because Osama bin Laden had provided the Chechen's with 30 million dollars worth of opium in exchange for a nuclear weapon- specifically Small Atomic Demolition Munitions (SADM) or suitcase nukes- as they are commonly called- or at least weapons grade WMD materials.[93]

In 1998, Congressman Curt Weldon examined former GRU Col. Stanislav Lunev's and Russian scientist Alexei Yablokov's testimony that a number of 10 kiloton SADM or suitcase nukes were missing from Russian stockpiles and that Russia had trouble keeping count of how many were actually made. Some were claimed to be hidden inside the U.S. according to Congressional testimonies in 1999.[94]

"Lunev defected to the United States in 1992 after working for more than a decade in the U.S. as a GRU operative.[95] Lunev participated in a GRU program collecting information on the President and senior U.S. political and military leaders so they

---

[93] Allison, Graham. Nuclear Terrorism: The Ultimate Preventable Catastrophe. New York: Times Books, 2004
[94] Symposium: Al Qaeda's Nukes by Jamie Glazov, FrontPage Magazine, October 27, 2006
[95] Stanislav Lunev. *Through the Eyes of the Enemy: The Autobiography of Stanislav Lunev*, Regnery Publishing, Inc., 1998. ISBN 0-89526-390-4

may be targeted for assassination in the event of war. According to Lunev, small man-portable nuclear weapons "that could be disguised to look like a suitcase" would be employed in a decapitating Russian attack against U.S. leaders and key communications and military facilities."[96]

Officially they were never found. The story was initially toned down as there was no significant evidence to point out the actual existence of the missing and hidden SADM's apart from testimonies of General Lebed, GRU Col Lunev and nuclear scientist Yablokov and other former high ranking GRU officer's. Alexander Lebed's testimony before Senator's Richard Lugar and Sam Nunn concerning lack of security over Russia's nuclear facilities resulted in the Luger Nunn nuclear non-proliferation agreement.[97]

The realistic notions above became a surrealistic nightmare when I went back through my files and found an article by the Atlanta Journal Constitution I had saved in June, 2000 about a Russian nuclear engineer residing in Atlanta, open and vulnerable to coercion, added to the frightening thought of these specific Chechens in town.

In June 21, 2000, an article in the Atlanta Journal Constitution was published profiling a Russian engineer. It described the engineer's background as having won a computerized visa lottery

---

[96] Ibid
[97] "Is Lebed Russia's Loosest Cannon? An Exclusive NBC interview with Alexander Lebed," October 2, 1997, http://www.msnbc.com

and that he, his wife and his two children were thrilled to be awarded with a new life in the land of opportunity. It also described that he was educated as a Russian nuclear engineer at the Moscow institute of engineering physics in 1980. In his new job in Atlanta, the Russian (nuclear) engineer worked for a software company, which produced, and maintained 3D development software for American nuclear and aerospace companies contracted with the government.[98]

The fact that he was a Russian nuclear engineer working for a foreign company residing in Atlanta, Georgia, that handled sensitive information on a national security scale, he was at a high risk of subversive manipulation by corrupt or criminal elements from Russia. His background automatically qualified him as a tempting asset to Russian organized crime groups and/or Russian intelligence agencies like Russian military intelligence GRU.[99] He most certainly would have been a high value target of their influence and manipulation in the future.

- Roughly 80% of all foreign companies in the Russian Federation are forced to pay a "Roof" by Krysha's (Organized Protection Rackets) for protection, according to the Center for Strategic and International Studies and various other experts on

---

[98] 'Russian engineer's move to U.S. is like a miracle' by Maria Mallory Atlanta Journal-Constitution, June 21, 2000.

[99] Emerging criminal state; Economic and Political Aspects of Organized Crime in Russia by Yuriy A. Voronin pg 56 - Russian Organized Crime; The new threat Edited by Phil Williams

Russian Organized Crime (ROC) and corruption. "Krysha's" most often target Russian employees and especially those in high management positions. Russian organized crime groups and individuals here in the U.S have most often targeted Russian Émigré's attempting to start fresh in the United States.[100]

- Atlanta had seen an escalation of approx. 50,000 Russian and Eurasian Émigrés since the mid 90's. Along with these émigrés, Russian criminals will usually follow.

- GRU, Russian Military Intelligence Directorate and brigades normally consist of twenty professional intelligence officers, subordinate to it. GRU specialists are directly responsible for the training and care of these brigades. The brigades are always on standby and ready for action as soon as they receive orders or command. Each of these conduct recruitment work among foreigners and Russian citizens, which could be used both in peacetime and in wartime in the intelligence interests of the front.[101]

This is why GRU intelligence officers Anton Surikov and Ruslan Saidov as Basaev's alleged GRU handlers played a critical role

---

[100] New York State Organized Crime Task Force, et al., "An Analysis of Russian Émigré Crime,"
Transnational Organized Crime 2(2-3) (Summer-Autumn 1996). Russian Organized Crime in The United States By James O. Finckenauer, Ph.D. International Center National Institute of Justice
[101] GRU (intelligence) http://warfare.ru

not to mention that they were later identified as two of the unidentified subjects present in Atlanta at the nightclub with the Chechens in a group across the bar the last night they were observed. The two un-subs were not mentioned in the report due to the fact that they could not be clearly identified by any pictures or other intelligence at that time.

Although there was nothing to indicate that the Russian nuclear engineer was a part of any conspiracy, he and his family were nonetheless in danger from people like these Chechens in particular. 911 demonstrated just how many lives terrorists were willing to take and maybe more.

The surrealistic circumstances with a Chechen warlord trained by the GRU with at least six of his men with a previous history in using nuclear materials as a means to threaten a population with nuclear terrorism and a history in hostage taking and a Russian nuclear engineer in the same city no more than half an hour's driving distance incited a horrific predicament that left me with sleepless nights. Even if I had non-official ranking or status within law enforcement or government, the accuracy of the reports with all the witnesses should have been sufficient credibility to initiate investigative attention to the matter. It should have given the authorities enough chilling feelings down their spine to follow up immediately, but with the exception of the efforts by my FBI contact that seemed paralyzed by the wall of bureaucracy, they just ignored the reports all together like they ignored so many other apparent warnings. I still tried to blow the whistle wherever I could blow it to no avail.

The timing between the report of the Chechen cross border and Cheney's rhetorical outbursts about terrorism and nuclear weapons and the growing cases of false flag and intelligence fabrications jump-started my concerns that they would try to use or twist my report for their dirty agendas. This is where Al Masry and his position as officer of the Chechnya branch of the Benevolence International Foundation and his liaison between Al Qaida and Hezbollah made this a realistic fact with concern with Cheney, the neocons and Israel's expansion of war with Iran. Bush, Cheney and the Neocons patterns of abuse seemed to read like a manual and usually started with the combination of their own behavior, rightwing media reports and plausibly deniable incidents like the latter. Due to these plausible predicaments I had sent in continuous letters to congress warning of such attempts from 2003 to 2007. I simply refused to accept my reports/memo's from being abused and did what I could to prevent something like that from happening by leaving official paper trails. Since the investigations into the intelligence fabrications were still fresh and that congress was stacked up over their heads in domestic and foreign issues, it would have been absurd to expect any form of response especially since I had a non official status as a civilian. However, they could not ignore or afford the possibility of serious consequences if my report had been abused in any way. Besides, the Democrats had plenty of demons in their closet too that they needed to cover up much like the Bush administration! Under the Clinton administration, there were many lapses and shady affairs that also allowed Al Qaida to gain strength such as the support for Kosovo Liberation Army (KLA) which was obviously a mutual understanding between Democrats and Republicans at the time.[102]

> "Loretta Napoleoni has argued that there is an Islamist drug route of al Qaeda allies across North Central Asia, reaching from Tajikistan and Uzbekistan through Azerbaijan and Chechnya to Kosovo.[i]
>
> This leads us to the paradoxical fact that in 1998 Clinton came to the support of the al Qaeda-backed Kosovo Liberation Army (KLA). He did so even though "[i]n 1998, the U.S. State Department listed the KLA ... as an international terrorist organization, saying it had bankrolled its operations with proceeds from the international heroin trade and from loans from known terrorists like Osama bin Laden."[ii]

According to congressional testimony by Ralph Mutschke from Interpol's Criminal Intelligence Directorate, a "significant amount" of KLA's source of financing from narcotics trafficking is in combination with terrorist activities.[103]

---

[102] Loretta Napoleoni, *Terror Incorporated: Tracing the Dollars Behind the Terror Networks* (New York: Seven Stories Press, 2005), 90-97

[103] Ralf Mutschke, "The Threat Posed by the Convergence of Organized Crime, Drugs Trafficking and Terrorism", statement before a hearing of the US House

Military Professional Resources, Inc. (MPRI), was sponsored with contracts by the U.S government to train KLA.[104] The State Dept had at one time labeled the KLA as a terrorist organization but retracted it later when the war in the region was over. KLA was also considered to be a criminal organization trafficking most of the heroin to Europe through Turkey.

DynCorp, a private military company (PMC) much like MPRI, were heavily engaged with the Kosovo Albanians and even the Serbs. DynCorp employees had been charged with numerous violations and investigated for a number of criminal actions such as slave/sex trade, forced prostitution of minors under ages of 15 during their presence in the Former Yugoslavia (Bosnia) and Iraq. Two of several whistleblowers that were fired had filed civil suits against DynCorp after reporting their cases of sex trade and sexual misconduct with minors to higher-ups. Ben Johnston, who reported DynCorp employees regularly buying under aged prostitutes, won his settlement in Fort Worth, Texas. Kathryn Bolkovac, a former UN Peacekeeper, investigating Eastern European slave market, was hired through contracts from her initial employer DynCorp to the U.N. When she uncovered and

---

of Representatives Committee on the Judiciary Subcommittee on Crime, December 13, 2000. Mr. Mutschke is the Assistant Director, Criminal Intelligence Directorate, International Criminal Police Organization - Interpol General Secretariat. Web site: http://www.house.gov/judiciary/muts1213.htm.

[104] THE PROGRESSIVE, August 1999, Title: "Mercenaries in Kosovo: The U.S. Connection to the KLA" Author: Wayne Madsen; COVERTACTION QUARTERLY, Spring-Summer 1999, Title: "Kosovo `Freedom Fighters' Financed by Organized Crime," Author: Michel Chossudovsky.

reported numerous U.N. police officers- who were also contracted from DynCorp- regularly visited clubs where they could buy forced sex also from girls under 15 years of age. One of the officers even bought a young girl for $6,000 for himself to keep locked up as a sex slave in his apartment. Bolkovac also won her case in Britain under U.K's, whistleblower statute -- the Public Interest Disclosure Act of 1998.[105]

Most of those involved in DynCorp sex slave scandals were sent home, some were fired. However NONE were prosecuted for their crimes.

Cases like these that make its way into the public limelight are only the tip of the iceberg. Nonetheless, these cases demonstrates the deep hypocrisy of the U.S, U.N and companies like DynCorp that are supposed to be instrumental in sustaining peacekeeping missions or other interventions into foreign conflicts. Whether it's U.N peacekeepers, NATO or other multinational military contingencies with private military companies are conditionally supplying, the psychological means for corruption and human rights violations to exist and increase and feed conditions for terrorism to take root.

While politicians hide behind the façade of democracy engulfing constituents with the promise of hope and prosperity, behind the curtain lurks the inevitable dark truth.

---

[105] Sex-slave whistle-blowers vindicated By Robert Capps

Hawk of Pandora

Democracy and hope? Where is real democracy? Harsh reality would say democracy has been driven into an artificial name especially within the years of the Bush era. During my life time the idea of democracy has had no balance jumping from hard left to hard right, administration after administration. Our foreign policies of intervention, whether it be imperialism or democratization, has failed to achieve its purpose due to the dark imbalances created by reckless policies. What seem to be successes of democracy are being replaced by behind the curtains corruption with main stream media blowing smoke screens while sweetening the honey for their stories.

Whistleblowers come out and throw the passionate die hard truth like a hard ball. Main stream media takes it and says "no fair it's too hard! We need to play fair! Let's play beach ball!"

Every one of those who say they stand for democracy but turn their heads against whistleblowers is superficially playing the tune of democracy which no longer defines its value of the idea while sustaining false hope riddled with dark realities.

Friedrich Nietzsche, wrote, On the History of Moral Feelings. "Hope. Pandora brought the jar with the evils and opened it. It was the gods' gift to man, on the outside a beautiful, enticing gift, called the 'lucky jar.' Then all the evils, those lively, winged beings, flew out of it. Since that time, they roam around and do harm to men by day and night. One single evil had not yet slipped out of the jar. As Zeus had wished, Pandora slammed the top down and it remained inside. So now man has the lucky jar in his house forever and thinks the world of the treasure. It is at his service; he reaches for it when he fancies it. For he does not know that the jar which Pandora brought was the jar of evils, and he takes the remaining evil for the greatest worldly good—it is hope, for Zeus did not want man to throw his life away, no matter how much the other evils might torment him, but rather to go on letting himself be tormented anew. To that end, he gives man hope. In truth, it is the most evil of evils because it prolongs man's torment."[106]

The point is that when governing politicians or corporations feed the rest of the people with an arbitrary purpose and hope they continue to covet the deep rooted issues of destructive elements that causes stalemate for fundamental solutions to evolve that would sustain a long term and genuine presence of hope.

We unfortunately live in a two faced generation that says one thing but does or cannot refrain from doing the other. Those who strive to maintain true faces, unfortunately face the corner of isolation because most people really can't handle the hard truth. The level of corruption cannot condone the other, however short and arbitrary the hopeful purposes we could look forward to there was still some difference in balanced achievements with the Democrats as there was affordable health care, and the economy got back on its feet which the Bush administration inherited a major national budget surplus of over $100 billion rather than the

---

[106] Nietzsche, Friedrich, *Human, All Too Human.* Cf. Section Two

catastrophic deficit of $1 trillion the Obama administration
inherited.

Even so, politically they were trying to win back Congress and the
presidential seat so they couldn't afford to ignore the possibility
of more intelligence reports being abused even if they refused to
acknowledge my letters. All that was needed was that these
possibilities were forwarded on record and that those in Congress
who were concerned about issues and situations like these would
bare these thoughts in the back of their minds. Thus temporarily
undermining any attempt to abuse reports like mine.

Patrons of Pandora

*"Know your enemy and know yourself and you can fight a
hundred battles without disaster." Sun Tzu*

After I had sent my reports to the FBI and no initial
investigation was undertaken, I realized that I also had to send this
to other experts. The FBI special agent I was in contact with had
been relocated by February 2001. My network of law enforcement
friends had enough to deal with trying to keep low profiles and
was stacked with their own cases. Among the experts I confided
to was "Bobby", an expert on Russian organized crime and author
of several successful books on intelligence and organized crime,
to get his expertise on the situation and what I should do. He
naturally recommended sending this to the authorities which had
already been done. Throughout the beginning of 2001until 911, I
had quite a few talks with Bobby basically on a moral level in
dealing with the overwhelming pressures of the situation. I can't
count how many times I was on the edge of frustration and
stressed to the peak.

Due to the lack of response, I then decided to send the reports in
different directions in order to make sure as many within federal
law enforcement agencies were made aware of these suspects, but
to no avail. I even faxed it off to Tampa, Florida's FBI field office
in light of the Superbowl. At that time I had no knowledge that
Mohammed Atta resided in Atlanta and had actually traveled

between Atlanta, Georgia and Tampa, Florida around the time before the Superbowl.

I felt compelled to do everything I possibly could to alert anyone that would care enough to do something apart from the special agent in Atlanta's effort to get a green light for the investigations. I was not officially contracted by any federal or local law enforcement so I was not affected by any bureaucracy or even "the wall." It was still extremely risky!

Considering the detailed report I had delivered regarding suspects identification supported by up close witness testimonies of at least a dozen witnesses, a witness report of a thirty minute conversation with the main suspect, identification of six other suspects from the same Interpol warrants and article with report on a Russian nuclear engineer, I was shocked at the lack of response to these suspects.

In the back of my mind I knew something was seriously wrong with the whole picture. I had sensitive knowledge of the widespread corruption in Atlanta. I knew who several of the organized crime players were and which establishments they were operating from. The Bush administration and its members had a crystal clear rotten history riddled with corruption and reckless policies with their aggressive Machiavellian approaches to domestic and foreign policies, such as their infamous involvement in the Iran Contra scandal, BCCI and other acts of crime. There was little chance that they would learn from lessons of the past and change to become better leaders or human beings.

Many of those convicted and involved in the Iran Contra scandal were appointed positions in the Bush administration. This notion would have serious effects on the heavy bureaucracy already existent from top to bottom of chains of command making any solid and effective decision makers counterproductive. With that in mind I knew that the bureaucracy within the Justice department would get worse than it was known to be. That alone told me there would be conflicting interests and that the integrity of these reports I delivered was not safe from any form of abuse, careerism or the possibility of corrupt involvement.

I made the choice to secure my reports by making as many copies I could afford, disengaged contact with my loyal colleagues and friends that knew about the suspects and were witnesses and notified as many other contacts about the report leaving too many loose ends and minimizing potentials for these reports to be abused. But the risk of abuse was still there. Eventually as light was shed on several of the cases from 911 and the Bush administration's abuse of other intelligence reports, much thanks to many of the other whistleblowers, I realized that I had made the right decision. These decisions I made were still major sins of bureaucracy, intelligence and underworld leaving me at dangerous risk of retaliation.

Patrons of Pandora

On August 30, 2001, I was supposed to meet a friend at a local alternative rock bar and ended up getting caught in a trap. That bar was one of the rock bars with several staff and guests suspected of being involved in local drug trafficking, distribution and other criminal activities. Their network included low level crews of soldiers and enforcers tied to the Kaplan crew and Capo "Mikey Scars" DiLeonardo from the Gambino crime family and some suspects from Russian/Israeli OC providing their criminal services insuring their own criminal investments using these bars and nightclubs as front companies. The same network where, my sources described, Russian goons would walk plain sight carrying briefcases handcuffed to their wrists in front of law enforcement officers in uniform working extra security shifts for one of these clubs. These officers also worked extra shifts in uniform for other clubs owned and operated by the same group of owners. It is important to note that Eastern European, Eurasian and Russian criminal émigrés often operate as ad hoc crews of enforcers or criminal entrepreneurs for hire with other organized crime groups (OCG's). They are also subject to paying percentages of their criminal profits to more powerful OCG's within their own ethnic criminal Diasporas.

While sitting at the bar drinking beverages I was approached by a loyal friend that asked me to go to the bathroom. He left to talk to some others. I took a few sips of my beer and went in to the bathroom. My friend followed. Immediately he told me I needed to get the hell out of there because there was a "crew" on their way to deal with me. This "crew," according to my friend heard within criminal circles, was going to teach me a permanent lesson. Despite my friend's warnings I stayed to find out who this crew was but called some other of my trusties for back up. I needed to get an idea of who these guys and their associates were. I was able to get hold of my close friends and colleagues of the network of officers and agents I knew I could trust to give them a heads up for back up. They knew what I stood for and what I was about.

Paul came inside to observe people in the backroom bar and the two others outside observing anyone coming in or out. After about fifteen minutes later "the crew" showed up. There were at least five other than their loyal partners in crime from the bar. Two of them went up to the bar and talked to one of the bar tenders involved. I recognized two of them from an earlier case involving a Russian and a "model" that was honey trapping on behalf of this criminal network. She was used to contact local businessmen and create situations where they could be blackmailed by these Russians. Kaplan's strippers from the Gold Club did exactly the same with businessmen visiting his club which was one of the reasons he was indicted. The Russian (Alex S) and the honey trap met at this same bar prior to my rough engagement with this same crew. The honey trap was closely associated to this crew which is what caught my interest to her in the first place. She was present when the crew attacked me. The Russian (Alex S), an independent operator and suspected money launderer for the local OC, had an office space in the same building as the public safety group I worked with. On one occasion, I had also observed him and his colleagues making a message drop off outside of a coffee shop in front of the same building. I sat drinking coffee outside with a view to either side. The two waiting for the drop off showed up few minutes earlier. These two guys looked like Russian goons with tattoos to match their rough appearances. Actually, one of them was identical to Anton Surikov and was also identical to one of the unidentified subjects (un-sub) at the Nightclub the last time we saw them. Surikov's identity as a un-sub became obvious several years later due to controversial media attention with photos of him and his partners. Still, Surikov's identity as the un-sub should be taken with a pinch of salt due to the fact that he was briefly noticed on two occasions without information or pictures of the un-sub to compare at the time to make any accurate account. The last night we observed the Interpol suspects at the club the intelligence officer and I briefly noticed the un-subs looking over at us together with the other Interpol suspects from the other side of the bar. They also made their associations obvious when they discussed and again pointed me out followed by the whole group playing a stare campaign with me across the bar island. The Interpol suspects were far more identifiable due to numerous close-up encounters- with multiple witnesses – identifying the main suspect and then the other suspects as a group with Interpol pictures available of each suspect as part of the same group added to the Interpol warrant of the main suspect (Basaev) and specific accounts of their behavior separately and among each other.

While they sat down to my left, Alex S the Russian and his partner showed up a few minutes later walking right past the guy that looked like Surikov and dropped a paper into his plastic bag without making any form of social contact with each other. The two that made the drop continued on and acted like nothing while the guys sitting next to me walked off in the other direction. These men were the people I suspected of being involved with the Serbian case concerning a Serbian suspect that established patterns linking Serbian organized crime and paramilitary group and its leader to the companies and banks controlled by Russian organized crime. Financial records from this case linked the case of the Bank of New York (BONY) scandal. There were at least four major leaders from Russian/Israeli organized crime involved with BONY; Yossif Kobzon (Council boss of Twenty First Century Association), Grigory Loutchansky (alleged crime boss and owner of Nordex), Semion Mogilevich (head of organization known as Red Mafia) and Sergei Mikhailov (head of Solntsevskaya). Berezovsky was also linked to BONY scandal.

Bank of New York's affiliations to Bank Menatep and other shadow banks were traced and listed in financial records I obtained from the Serbian case was separate from the BONY case but made clear cut links with the BONY trail of banks involved.

Many of the players with the Bank of New York (BONY) money laundering scandal also had the same BCCI players written all over it. Several banks in Atlanta that were used during the BCCI and Iran Contra days were also involved. It is highly plausible that this same network may have also aided the Chechens in Atlanta considering Adnan Khashoggi's influence within the BCCI network and his business ties to Berezovsky, Khoz Noukhaev and Ibn al Khattab. (see ref. footnote 61 "In spring 1997 Adnan Khashoggi introduced Khoz-Ahmed Noukhaev to James Baker.")

"BCCI's activities in Atlanta and its acquisition of the National Bank of Georgia through First American;

Although the Justice Department's indictments of Clark Clifford and Robert Altman cover portions of how BCCI acquired National Bank of Georgia, other important allegations regarding the possible involvement of political figures in Georgia in BCCI's activities there remain outside the indictment. These allegations, as well as underlying facts regarding BCCI's activities in Georgia, require further investigation."[107]

Since my actions of exposing the Chechens consisted of sustaining contact with the suspects, gathering witness testimonies and following up with other actions to identify other target suspects and then reporting it to the FBI would normally be considered case officer or agent tasks. My function was simply an unsolicited volunteer that happened to expose suspects tied to Al Qaida or even other enemies, took testimonies, followed up to gather what I could, wrote a report and reported it in to the FBI. Because the Chechen case would have been considered a major issue handled by high level officers or intelligence officials especially dealing with the plausibility of nuclear terrorism by these Chechens, I was definitely an interesting low level unsolicited volunteer for them to note. There would be no mistaking of any foreign intelligence like the Russian GRU, Mossad or even domestic intelligence agency cliques curiosity to the Chechen case even if I was a non-official operator.

The fact about the Chechen case was a non official situation where we noticed the suspects and did something about it in the spur of the moment. There was no official unit behind it; it was handled outside of traditional local or federal law enforcement context or structure. There was no command structure behind the decisions. I was never paid-monetary or otherwise - for my involvement. It was "do something or a lot of people are going to get hurt or die" way of handling it with a lot of improvising care

---

[107] The BCCI Affair; A Report to the Committee on Foreign Relations United States Senate by Senator John Kerry and Senator Hank Brown December 1992 102d Congress 2d Session Senate Print 102-140
http://www.fas.org/irp/congress/1992_rpt/bcci/

and consideration for the immediate people at risk while legally reporting it to the FBI and other authorities so they could continue where we started off. But they didn't despite efforts by the agent I was in contact with.

Throughout 2000 to 2001, there were numerous events and reports of Israeli students squandering about selling art work in conspicuous manners and apparently taking photos and infiltrating government buildings in Atlanta. They were exposed as Israeli intelligence by DEA during the summer of 2001 operating around the country and had been operating within the country since 1999 and in Atlanta from early 2000.[108] From many of the reports about the Israeli students it would seem like they were literally testing security and also infiltrating for purposes of protecting their own assets. While patrolling several of the federal buildings, I had also paid notice to small student groups who had taken "waist shot" pictures of security around the federal buildings; specifically, a group of four with one filming with his camcorder towards the Federal building from below his waist line. This student used exactly the same method I used during my time

---

[108] The Israeli "art student" mystery; For almost two years, hundreds of young Israelis falsely claiming to be art students haunted federal offices -- in particular, the DEA. No one knows why -- and no one seems to want to find out. By Christopher Ketcham, Salon.com
http://www.salon.com/news/feature/2002/05/07/students/print.html

at the academy when they tested us in counter surveillance. I took waist shots of the mock "terrorist" crew that had us under surveillance during field exercises. The mock crew was experienced veterans from intelligence and law enforcement. I took a picture of all three without them knowing I had pictures of them while they had us under surveillance. This is how I knew this guy was definitely taking pictures of the federal building which was reported to their security. After that I had checked around and heard that there were some students from Israel and the Mideast studying at some of the schools in downtown and midtown Atlanta.

It would not be unlikely that some of the "art students" had picked up on me when I noticed them. They especially needed to be wary of getting caught and noticed me when I paid attention to them. Most of these students must have come straight out of intelligence school without picking up field experience because they stuck out like sore thumbs too many times. There were many suspicious reports about them from wary law enforcement and federal agents which lead to their apprehension and scandal in the first place. The "art students" seemed to operate aggressively, sporadic and too congestive which meant that they were under serious time constraints and knew something was going to happen soon and needed very quick results. Since the Israelis were reported to have tracked 911 suspects in Florida they would have had some knowledge about the Chechens or perhaps Atta's activities in Atlanta. Also considering that several of their citizens like Boris

Berezovsky and other wealthy Jewish businessmen from the
Caucasus were heavily into supporting Chechens like Basaev and
Noukhaev, they would have clear interests in keeping an eye on
these shady assets. As an Israeli citizen, Berezovsky's interests by
financing numerous Chechen operations including the Dagestan
invasion in 99 and giving two million dollars to Shamil Basaev in
97 under normal circumstances would have qualified him as a
sponsor of terrorism and could have caused Israeli's problems.[109]

With Chechen Interpol suspects in Atlanta, it is reasonable to
believe that Mossad would have had a few of their agents there
too to keep an eye on what was happening. They knew something
big was about to happen. This was definitely a rush job
considering that Israeli intelligence and military are known for
being meticulous planners and operators.

The intelligence field is a strange world because you can walk
down a crowded street and walk past thousands of normal average
people and then in the midst there is that one or two individuals
that stick out no matter how much they try to fit in. You just feel
them. You know they are either intelligence or special operations
or law enforcement. Even criminals, especially members of
organized crime and terrorists, give off a certain demeanor or
attitude that make them stick out in some way from the average
person just like the Chechens at the nightclub. It's like a keen

---

[109] *Russian Says Kremlin Faked 'Terror Attacks' By PATRICK E. TYLER
Published: February 1, 2002 NY Times*

sense of knowing much like the scents that animals give off or notice. However, that is not enough to suspect someone of committing any crime or doing something wrong. It takes a lot more direct and specific information to make any accurate account of criminal, intelligence or terrorist related analysis.

"Often the Israeli "students" sold their artwork on street locations near federal buildings. In one incident in Atlanta, they showed up outside an unlisted FBI office and began taking photos, according to sources. Agents collared them and sent them on their way."[110]

It was also suggested that the Israelis were conducting counter terrorism investigations inside the United States.

Carl Cameron from Fox News that blew the Israeli spy ring story wide open divulged in the backing of Israelis that: "There is no indication that the Israelis were involved in the 9-11 attacks, but investigators suspect that the Israelis may have gathered intelligence about the attacks in advance, and not shared it."[111]

That is most likely true; to protect the Jewish citizens in Atlanta or elsewhere.

If the Israelis were conducting counter terrorism surveys checking weak links in the security, this would have been how they would do it. Israeli intelligence had given prior warning to U.S

---

[110] The spies who came in from the art sale *Creative Loafing* has obtained a report detailing alleged Israeli spy activity in the United States. Published 03.20.02 By John Sugg Creative Loafing, Atlanta.

[111] Ibid

authorities about a potential major attack. Considering Mossad and Israelis' reputation for proactive measures before terrorists incidents happen, it would not be surprising that they would have sent a number of their agents in to the U.S. to do their own intelligence gathering. Israelis have always been diehard about protecting their own and will do it at whatever cost.

It's no surprise that their presence would raise a lot of suspicion of different conspiracies given the fact that numerous rotten apples within the Israeli government, military, intelligence, Russian Jewish émigré members of OC, like Berezovsky, and other networks such as the Israeli Turkish networks have dirt hidden in their closets for supporting terrorism. Under separate investigations by both the FBI, which Sibel Edmonds worked on translating evidence, and CIA's front company Brewster Jennings that was exposed before 911 and Valerie Plame's outing by the Cheney cabal, there were serious allegations that Israeli and Turkish "rotten" interests were involved with selling U.S nuclear secrets to AQ Khans networks and then possibly to terrorist groups like Al Qaida or even the Chechens. This would be a major motive for Israelis to cover for rogue transactions to terrorists that would lead to more anti Semitism and loss of support from the U.S.

Israel had allowed and given free passage to many Russian Jewish émigré's throughout the years. Many of these, being Russian organized crime figures, were given Israeli passports no questions asked. Yossif Kobzon, Grigory Loutchansky (owner of Nordex alleged by Interpol as a front for organized crime investigated for selling nuclear proponents to countries like Iran), Grigory Lerner (*The Jerusalem Post* 12 Feb. 1998; Xinhua 10 June 1997), Semion Mogilevich (head of organization known as Red Mafia [Robert Friedman]), Vyacheslav Ivankov and Sergei Mikhailov (head of Solntsevskaya used a fake passport but has not been pursued) were among the heavyweight of Russian Israeli organized crime figures and have criminal operations in Israel, mainly Tel Aviv.[112] Many of these have also been involved in trafficking and selling arms to Israel's enemies such as Iran, Iraq and Syria and arms that have made its way to terrorist groups; Al Qaida, Hamas, Hezbollah, Islamic Jihad, PFLP, and PFLP-GC. These Russian Jewish émigré's identified as organized crime members are heavily involved in the woman sex slave market. A number of these women have ended up being trained as honey traps operating as female spies for rogue intelligence crews, organized crime and terrorist affiliated organizations. It is highly plausible that some of these students were spying on behalf of these networks especially since the DEA was also targeted due to their investigations on Russian/Israeli organized crime groups trafficking ecstasy into Atlanta, Georgia and elsewhere along the east, mid and west coast. One of the major suppliers of ecstasy was a Jewish American from New York associated to Kaplan

---

[112] *Red Mafiya: How the Russian Mob Has Invaded America* (Boston: Little Brown & Co., 2000

crew of the Gambino crime family and tied to the ad hoc network in Atlanta. The Kaplan case showed how they used strippers as honey pots for criminal purposes to influence professional sports athletes' and events. These honey pots could easily serve as smokescreens for intelligence collection and criminal purposes since organized criminals from Russia and Eastern Europe are multifaceted opportunists.[113]

Several of the honey pots I came across had been operating on behalf of Russian organized crime operating out of Belgrade, Israel and Hungry.

In1999, I was engaged with a case where a female agent from the Balkans called Sasha attempted to recruit me by charm, seduction and different offers to help her spy on her boyfriend who was a top management executive in a family owned pharmaceutical company that specialized in cosmetic pharmaceutical products. Her cover plan was to infiltrate by marriage with this business owner. Her excuse for needing my help was that she wanted to find out why he was keeping her in the dark about his companies secrets by finding information from his home and office. My suspicion began here! As soon as she offered me a job in her father's Security Company in Belgrade, Yugoslavia, red alarms started going off in my head. When she gave me a T-shirt from her father's security company with the

---

[113] Le Monde, Paris

logo of a Tiger I instantly knew she was trying to recruit me for something that was a serious felony offense and on behalf of a Serbian group or groups involved with organized crime and paramilitary activities that used the logo of the Tiger. Her attempt to recruit me annoyed the hell out me or outright pissed me off! The notion that any person or people with criminal intents think they can manipulate me into taking part in their criminal offenses and betray my principles and country is a serious insult to me. I didn't need any more motives to find out more about the criminal intents of this woman regardless of whether she was acting on behalf of organized criminal or terrorist thugs. In this case it was both. The name of the security company her father was an executive in was affiliated by business and members with a group called Serb Volunteer Guard also known as "Arkan's White Tigers" run by a former Serbian paramilitary leader Zeljko "Arkan" Raznjatovic. I was already familiar with Arkan due to his activities in Norway and Sweden. Many of Arkan's criminal business networks stretched from members of his "White Tigers" through his 'business' partners. These businesses varied from a professional soccer club, night clubs to fuel racketeered gas stations to his business partners Security Company and international businesses using the same brand name and logo of the tiger. Arkan was one of the most feared and ruthless gangster, paramilitary leader and politician in Serbia. The logo of the tiger in Serbia was exclusive to Arkan's White Tigers and anyone within the country using this logo and brand name for their business would have needed Arkan's express permission with interests as informal 'investor' in their company. Because Arkan already had a very bad reputation across Europe many of these companies could not officially be affiliated to him and as with most heads of organized crime groups they naturally use others to facilitate operations of their companies. There were several people close to Arkan's inner circle of associates that were owners and managers with the companies using the tiger as the brand name and logo. The relative of one of Arkan's top ranking officers in the paramilitary group was an executive officer running one of these companies from an office in London, England. The company owned by Sasha's boyfriend's family also had their main research laboratory in the neighboring business district in London as the company using the tiger brand name and logo.

Arkan was a diehard fan and leader of the fan club for Belgrade's pro football (soccer) team Red Star for which he recruited most of the men for his White Tigers.[114] Arkan eventually bought ownership of a soccer club in Belgrade which later became a top league club in Serbia Montenegro.[115] The security company was responsible for security for Arkan's football (soccer) club FK Obilić in Belgrade. This coincided with Sasha's bragging that the

---

[114] Football Hooligans, and War", Ivan Čolović, Central European University Press, 2000.
[115] Official site for Obilić fans, http://home.drenik.net/vitezovi/

security company her 'father' worked for was responsible for security for Belgrade's professional soccer team.

Arkan had several warrants for his arrest by International War Crimes Tribunal for his group's involvement of genocide. Interpol and European warrants from 7 countries including Belgium, Netherland (Holland), Germany, Norway and Sweden included robbery, arms sales and murder charges. He had been a career criminal and graduated to assassin from the mid seventies to the 90's.[116] He was also convicted and spent several terms in European prisons. He was also famous for escaping almost every prison in Europe.[117] Arkan was assassinated January 15, 2000, at the Intercontinental Hotel in Belgrade by a guard from the mobile brigade and two others. The assassin was said to have been tied to the underworld and that Slobodan Milosevic was said to have been behind the assassination. The Milosevic theory carries a strong plausibility because Arkan competed in the underworld with Slobodan Milosevic's son Marko Milosevic who wanted Arkan out of the way. Arkan's nightclub and underworld businesses were much more successful in Belgrade while Marko's Nightclub and his other businesses were going bankrupt.[118] They also had conflicts over rival bootleg gas market in Belgrade.

---

[116] A Shady Militia Chief Arouses Serbs By CHUCK SUDETIC, New York Times Published: Sunday, December 20, 1992
[117] "Gangster's life of Serb warlord" By Balkans correspondent Paul Wood BBC News Saturday, 15 January, 2000
[118] Profile: Marko Milosevic, BBC News Monday, 9 October, 2000

Another motive was that Arkan knew too much about Milosevic's crimes and due to political pressures from the international community Milosevic had many motives to get rid of Arkan. Many of Arkan's most loyal high ranking officers were being professionally assassinated one after the other and Arkan's business and political alliances began resenting Arkan's power and used close associates to assassinate him on behalf of all of the above. The Serbian newspaper Politika daily wrote that Arkan knew his assassins and spoke with them prior to killing him. [Politika Daily, 2000]

Apart from her suspicious excuses of his affairs and "dishonesty", the information Sasha was apparently interested in was about the business affairs of his company virtually to the point of obsession. She was highly interested in the chemical 'recipes' they used for their "revolutionary" product and enthusiastic about telling the little she knew about it. According to Sasha, the chemical (neurotransmitters) or biotechnology they used were supposed to increase or regenerate dying cells within the skin. This clearly fascinated her. She made it obvious that she was pissed and in despair that her boyfriend would not share that with her. The more she tried to play me with crocodile tears and emotional displays, the more she actually exposed herself. Despite her beauty and compelling charm, she literally thought she had me wrapped around her finger while I played along collecting as much information as I legally could. She would continuously imply that she could help me with different offers if I would help her. She had also tried to drag a girl I call April in my neighborhood, a beautiful woman that I had become well acquainted with, into the intrigues. It was in fact a result of their so called friendship that I met Sasha. April was a former model and nude dancer from a strip club that was tied to the mob. Both April and Sasha flaunted their sexuality with a clear purpose of manipulation. April was pretentiously unaware of what was really happening.

I was once told by a wise friend of mine that a man's courage comes from his wits and grace, not from his balls and boner. This is true, but all too often men go around thinking with their balls and boner as a supplement to their courage and pride. Many women find this quality as an aspect for manipulation and vulnerability of men and use that as an excuse to abuse as well. This is why honey traps or female agents are able to seduce, extract information or set up the men or women they target for failure.

These two women carried on their games and intrigues to the point where they were making things obvious. Sasha had even introduced me to her boyfriend. He was clearly infatuated with Sasha. That wasn't surprising given her beauty and seductive charm. Throughout the first month she kept trying to convince either April or I about her boyfriend keeping her in blind but it didn't have much effect on me. I kept adding up the information.

One thing was clear, Sasha was in search of industrial secrets from her boyfriends' business, and it had to do with the chemical/biotech they used for their pharmaceutical product. From Sasha's frustration, it seemed that her boyfriend and family had good procedures keeping that information tight. In Sasha's case, considering her desperation to get that information, I believe that she was under a lot of pressure. She had a daughter that was still with her "family." Her family was apparently involved with a Serbian criminal/paramilitary organization accused of genocide. Women from the slave trade are often forced to spy. In many cases, their family members, as in Sasha's case, her daughter, are used as collateral (hostage) to get them to cooperate. Sasha showed clear indications of natural motherly fear in regards to her daughter. If they don't, their family members are sometimes killed. Sasha's daughter could have been sold to the black market if they thought they could get a good price for her. That is the brutal reality of the underworld in the sex slave industry. In this sense it became a profoundly difficult predicament about what to do. I had contacted a few friends of mine from special operations, State Dept and my former instructor (U.N WMD/terrorism expert) who had a lot of experience with these matters. It needed to be handled very low key without alerting this girl or her handlers that they were exposed and without placing her daughter at risk. The rest was handled by government. How I don't know but whatever operation this suspect was up to was clearly burned. It wasn't long after this that Arkan was killed.

When honey traps or female agents are used to infiltrate a company, organization or individuals, it is usually the first step to get someone on the inside. Honey traps are very cost effective; costing nothing for intelligence, criminal or terrorist organizations by planting their low cost spies on targets. They are also considered to be immune from any form of prosecution because in most occasions it is impossible to catch them committing a crime. Using sex or seduction to fool people to reveal secrets or set up the target for extortion is not against the law unless authorities can prove that the honey trap is actually operating on behalf of a foreign intelligence agency, organized crime or a terrorist group and they have to actually be in the process of doing something illegal. Most of their activities are based on either establishing contact- many times sexual- and setting their targets up for scandals, for distractions or simply take part in retaliation tactics with smear campaigns and such to ruin their targets' lives. They are also known to target investigators with sensitive knowledge of their organization's illicit operations by setting them up for entrapments which is also impossible to prove. This leaves their handlers and organizations they work for untouched by exposure. Honey traps are mostly self reliant earning their own way by prostitution or as dancers at strip clubs or other criminal schemes of emotional exploitation. Internet dating schemes are clear indications of this. Several known honey traps especially from east Europe, Russia and Africa have been displayed through pictures contacting men through dating sites by email. The men they come in contact with are literally seduced over the internet and get suckered into sending money for a plane ticket or helping these lovely ladies they never met out of a so called 'crisis.' I recognized a few of these honey traps on online dating scheme register websites. They managed to lure at least a dozen men to send $750 to $1000 for plane tickets or other reasons within two weeks earning roughly 10,000 easy dollars. These men would often send money for plane tickets thinking they would finally get to meet the woman of their dreams. If a handler operates a dozen women on dating schemes, that is a criminal operation worth millions of dollars a year.

Another reason for using these dating sites is that they can lure businessmen or exploitable individuals to operate unwittingly for favors on their behalf. Blackmail snares are also set up through dating sites.

Honey traps always have handlers. In Sasha's case, it may have been her "father." Honey traps are known to call their handlers as "father" or "uncle." Once they have gathered the basics or even sensitive information that handlers believe they can use, the handler sends in someone better trained and experienced at espionage or intelligence gathering that is placed to get more sensitive data. Sasha's objective may have been a first phase of getting on the inside. The information in this case was bio and chemical components and composition of the products.

Bio and chemical composition and technology in western companies have always been attractive targets for eastern European intelligence, organized crime and terrorist organizations. Bio or chemical agent components targeting neurotransmitters is the main idea for producing chemical nerve agents like BZ, Sarin or VX gas. I don't know how important the product secrets of Sasha's boyfriend's company and its composites were? What relevance these secrets had to the group she was involved with or how they would be able to use those secrets? I am no WMD expert, however, it doesn't take a genius to understand that a person operating or spying on behalf of a paramilitary group wanted for genocide and was under an investigation for using nerve agents, their interests in the companies' neuro component secrets were not because they wanted to look great.[119] The academy I was trained at, and one of my instructors who was a WMD expert and inspector for the United Nations and International Atomic Energy Agency (IAEA), taught me enough to know that the situation with these suspects' interest in neuron technology was distinctive and serious enough not to ignore. This Serb group may have wanted to gain favor for more Russian support by passing these secrets on to Russian

---

[119] Serbs 'used chemical weapons' As British team unearths growing number of atrocities, UN adviser alleges 4,000 Albanians poisoned. by Richard Norton-Taylor and Lucy Ward, The Guardian, Tuesday 24 August 1999 01.45 BST

intelligence and rogue scientists who could use it to develop new or enhanced strains of nerve agents. What I did know, Sasha had an unhealthy or dangerous interest for accessing industrial secrets and was willing to break laws to get it. Her statements about her "father's" employer or company clearly indicated that it was controlled by Zeljko Arkan Raznjatovic. She had also confessed her strong views regarding Arkan as being a Serbian national hero.

Western intelligence agencies feared that groups in former Yugoslavia had access to WMD materials and especially bio or chemical weapons that would be used for ethnic cleansing like the Nazis used gas to kill Jews in the masses. In fact, a U.N investigating adviser and toxicologist said that Serb groups had already used Sarin gas against several thousands, mostly children, in Kosovo and also found traces of BZ gas among the victims. The report of Serbs' use of nerve agents was also followed by an investigation by the FBI.[120] Serbian military already had large amounts of BZ, Sarin and other incapacitating agents available with the complements from Russia. Arkan had a close relationship with and support from the ultra nationalist Duma member Vladimir Zhirinovsky in Russia.[121] In one incident involving collaborating evidence of threats using WMD devices, Arkan had threatened NATO with using Russia's alleged super secret

---

[120] Ibid

weapon "the Elipton" provided by Vladimir Zhirinovsky.[122] There is no evidence of the weapon Elipton's actual existence other than the threats that were made. Arkan was already wanted for committing genocide. The paramilitary groups on both sides had already committed genocide by the thousands and fears that nerve agents to commit more genocide were paramount. Arkan was certainly a tyrant leader that would have no arguments or reluctance with using nerve agents against Albanian, Bosnian or Croatian Muslims.

The intelligence report I wrote which was delivered in 1999 concerned Sasha, the company her father worked for and the Russians, was composed of transcripts of records of banks and companies leaving an obvious picture of money laundering operations that corresponded with the BONY trail of banks. It was after that that the Russians tried to place another honey trap on me.

The Russian honey trap number I witnessed meeting at the bar with Alex and his crooked patrons or street hoods were the same that had ambushed me once before after I inquired about her at one of the night clubs these people were associated to. I used a picture of the honey trap I took while I was at her place the same night she approached me, after her meeting with the Russian,

---

[121] Serbs threaten to unleash deadly 'secret weapon' ROBERT BLOCK in Belgrade, The Independent *Tuesday, 15 February 1994*
[122] Ibid

made her easily recognizable by the staff at the 'shady' clubs. This was the staff that tipped off the crew that targeted me. Nevertheless, her intentions for approaching me were not legit and under instructions by the Russian she met at the bar. Remembering what happened during after I was ambushed became blurry because I was knocked out and I ended up in the hospital looking like a truck hit me. But I knew these guys were the ones who attacked me because they had approached me about the honey pot in a threatening manner right before I was attacked. I knew these guys at the bar were not friendly. The way they placed themselves in the backroom where I stood sipping my coke, it was obvious their intentions were to insure I did not leave without them as escorts, and apparently the idea was for them to escort me somewhere or repeat the same with fatal consequences. What they did not know was I had back up by colleagues I trusted. My colleague and friend inside gave them the impression that there was more backing me up. Their expression was quite clear by looking at each other that whatever idea they had in mind was a very bad idea and apparently changed their plans and eventually left. The following week three planes hit the twin towers and the Pentagon September 11, 2001.

When those planes hit the world trade center and the pentagon on 9/11 and everything that happened before that, I knew that the psychological war of blowing the whistle was only the beginning and was going to get worse. From the warnings I got from an FBI agent, Bobby, other friends within local and federal law enforcement, advised me to relocate, change my name or certainly keep a low profile because my life was at risk, especially after the incident at the bar the week prior to 9/11. They knew that things were going to get very messy with the aftermath of 9/11. Despite the appreciated support by friends and colleagues, it was clear that even they would have limitations in covering my back because the situation was getting too dangerous and financing and official support was lacking. The only thing I could do was get the hell out of Dodge and leave whatever I had behind.

Uniformed Negligence

"Altruism, compassion, empathy, love, conscience, the sense of justice -- all of these things, the things that hold society together, the things that allow our species to think so highly of itself, can now confidently be said to have a firm genetic basis. That's the good news. The bad news is that, although these things are in some ways blessings for humanity as a whole, they didn't evolve for the "good of the species" and aren't reliably employed to that end. Quite the contrary: it is now clearer than ever (and precisely *why*) the moral sentiments are used with brutal flexibility, switched on and off in keeping with self interest; and how naturally oblivious we often are to this switching. In the new view, human beings are a species splendid in their array of moral equipment, tragic in their propensity to misuse it, and pathetic in their constitutional ignorance of the misuse." [from *The Moral Animal*] Robert Wright

At the nightclub where these suspects had been identified there were uniformed officers working as extra security that were entirely disinterested in taking even the simplest form constructive action such as observe, identify and report. The mere fact of law enforcement officers working in uniform as extra security left no doubt that these officers were being outsourced for private contracts in government uniforms. Whether many claim it was legal, others claimed this was corrupt. Several private security companies in Atlanta that have outsourced uniformed police officers have been investigated for corruption.

Nearly every officer I knew of worked extra shifts as security or other type of jobs, most of course legal and out of uniform. When you need to make money, a living and pay those bills and so on, you work extra shifts. That is just a fact of life! Besides, the majority of good law enforcement officers who are straight, honest and without a single hint of being corrupt, should never be singled out due to rotten apples often laying dark shadows over the rest of the department. Unfortunately they do!

However, there is a clear legal line between outsourcing law enforcement in uniform for private contracts and law enforcement officers taking extra shifts out of uniform. As soon as that line has been broken, those who crossed that line including the officers taking extra shifts in uniform for private contracts- innocent or not- are placed in serious issues of legal conflicts of interest. The bottom line is whether they are a cop inside or outside the uniform; they represent law enforcement and should not be placed into situations that prevent them from serving the purpose of law enforcement and serving the public.

Good officers usually consider it a privilege and honor to serve and rightfully so! Unfortunately, being law enforcement in any city or suburbia can often be a quagmire. You did not have to do anything wrong and police would be politically pinned with criticism. Law enforcement everywhere often seems to be a pincushion for political cannon fodder. It goes with the job! Law enforcement wages in Atlanta or many other places were not much to brag about either. The morale was very difficult to keep balanced. These attributes are often the foundations of cultivating corruption.

Nevertheless, this dubious outsourcing raised substantial quagmires of law enforcements ability to resist, react or respond to crime and especially higher end corruption or even terrorist cases without causing alarmist issues of their suspect extra jobs or earnings.

"Many people in big cities don't trust the cops because of corruption. When people see law enforcement officers working as bouncers at local mobbed up night clubs and restaurants the credibility of trust naturally vanishes."[123]

The manager at the nightclub where the suspects were observed stated that he didn't trust the officers that worked extra security at the nightclub. The nightclub itself was never under suspicion of being mobbed up despite a number of their mobbed up guests which is why it was a good place for research on a behavioral factor. The research was based on specific behavior characteristics of organized criminals that stick out compared to the general public.

What was certain they, the uniformed officers, couldn't do in regards to the Chechen suspects was going in to even question or

---

[123] Robert I. Friedman, *Red Mafiya: How the Russian Mob Has Invaded America* (Boston: Little Brown, 2000)

put the handcuffs on these guys due to the Interpol warrants. No one really knew how many of these guys were there. You put the handcuffs on one of them, it could have sparked a major hostage situation in the nightclub itself.

At a nightclub in Oslo, Norway, the police surrounded a nightclub full of "English soccer hooligans" with riot police during a world cup qualifying soccer match between Norway and England played in Oslo. When a few officers came over with authoritarian attitudes and when they put handcuffs on one of the English soccer fans while standing outside with a beer in his hand it triggered a major riot with the other fans and they completely went ballistic. They threw chairs and tables out of the windows and totaled the place for tens of thousands of dollars in damages. That one step between diplomacy and aggressive action can be enough to trigger or prevent catastrophic consequences. Luckily, no one was seriously hurt. Norwegian law enforcement are known to be highly effective in most occasions when they have the support to do the job they are good at. The nightclub incident was one of those instances where they underestimated the audacity, toughness and loyalty of the English soccer fans.

The same applied in this situation with the exception that these suspects have been previously involved in disastrous hostage incidents where hundreds of people have been killed including children.

This is why I knew not to provoke these suspects with any aggressive tones, but just enough to get them to react to expose themselves.

These suspects were well rehearsed and accustomed to hostage taking. Budenovsk, Beslan, the Moscow theatre and numerous other hijackings and assaults accredit their fierce savvy and notorious ability for taking from hundreds to over a thousand hostages at a time with results of bloodshed in the end much due to the Russians' aggressive handling of the situation. There is no winning when situations like that first take its course.

Sun Tzu (mythical and legendary inspiration behind "the Art of War") described a story that modern leaders should learn from, especially the Israelis and Russians in regards to their ways of dealing with Chechens and Palestinians. This lesson was suited for concern of the situation at the nightclub in regards to the Beslan and Budenovsk tragedies.

"In 206 B.C., Cao Cao (155-220), a great statesman, artist of war and man of letters, led his army to attack the city of Huguan. As the city was strategically located and very difficult to access, Cao's army could not take it in spite of great efforts. Cao got extremely outraged and said, "Once I get into the city, I will have all those in it buried alive." Soon his words were spread throughout the city. As the defenders in the city feared that it would really happen to them, they waged a desperate resistance. As a result, Cao's army found it even harder to win the battle. They made months of attempts to get in but in vain. Cao became more uneasy and consulted with his generals for a scheme.

At a meeting, General Cao Ren rose from his seat and said, "The art of war tells us that we should not put the enemy in too tight a ring that the enemy should be left a way to survive. But now we have been trapping our enemy in a deadly corner. What's more, you have declared to have them all buried alive. This will only make them battle desperately against us, for they would rather fight to death than be buried alive. As I estimate, the enemy has almost run out of supplies. If we now give them a ray of hope by leaving an open in the ring, they are very likely to surrender to us, for they would rather survive than fight to death for nothing.

Cao Cao thought the idea quite sensible and ordered to do as the general said. As had been expected, the defending troops in the city soon crossed over to Cao's side. The city was finally seized without a cruel fight. "[124]

Sun Tzu's punch line, "Do not thwart an enemy retreating home. If you surround the enemy, leave an outlet; do not press an enemy

---

[124] BRADFORD, Alfred S. *With Arrow, Sword, and Spear: A History of Warfare in the*
Ancient World. Westport, Conn.: Praeger, 2001.

that is cornered. These are the principles of warfare." Sun Tzu. [125]

Never press an enemy too hard into a corner for they will become unpredictably aggressive. Predictability is key to victory!

The predictability of any covert operational cell or team is that once exposed or as they say in the intelligence field "burned," the likely outcome is that the operation disengages or they risk further exposure and chances for apprehension increases. Therefore I had the advantage given their need for covert discretion. The Chechen suspects made serious mistakes and their vulnerability was their pride. In regards to these specific Interpol suspects they were itching to hint who they were. They wanted people to know who they were. It was their weakness. This also made them dangerous and eager to act in a big way.

In 1999, Khoz-Ahmed Noukhaev, the Chechen warlord and leader of the Chechen criminal community 'Obshina' showed the same clear symptoms as the suspects at the nightclub in his documentary film about him. He took a lot of pride expressing himself as the 'head' leader of Chechen resistance and Chechen criminal community. He openly described how he had to build 'his' army and set up a Chechen criminal community based on the "same way mafia groups were set up in Moscow."

Basaev himself also loved the limelight expressing his pride when he allowed himself and his group to be televised live on Russian

---

[125] "Art of War" Sun Tzu; Translated from the Chinese by Lionel Giles, M.A. (1910)

TV during the Budenovsk raid.[126] Shamil and his top crew were not wearing hoods. For him it was important not to mask his identity. He wanted the world to know that he was the greatest Chechen warrior of modern times. His pride stood out like a sore thumb. This is why he stood out from the average person walking down the street and especially among other people within the nightclub when I stood face to face with him and when my partner had a discussion with him. Basaev hated playing incognito. Shamil Basaev continued to demonstrate this particular flamboyant ego when he notified Russian media about a canister of radiological material cesium in Ismailovsky Park, Moscow. When the suspect, Basaev, at the nightclub opened himself up to my partner, he was hinting at the extravagant acts of consequences he as a warrior would incur upon his enemies. He had a dire need to hint to my partner that he was a diehard warrior willing to sacrifice himself for his men.

Some of the other Interpol suspects also expressed this same behavior as one of them had described to a woman where he was from. Again his pride hinted and exposed his identity from the Caucasus.

Another suspect within the group of suspects also made apparent reactions of behavior revealing the group.

Since I was unarmed it was important to leave them with the perception that I was not alone. At the bar, while viewing the un-

---

[126] Yeltsin draws bitter wrath of Chechens, CNN, April 22, 1996

named picture of Shamil Basaev while suspect Edisoultanov stood next to me and stared on and off at the picture, he knew that his boss had been exposed and that the group he was with was also at risk of being burned. While I was at the bar a friend came up behind me and asked if I was ok. I showed him five fingers pointing upstairs to let him know where the other five suspects were. He passed quick enough into the crowd so that he was not identified by the suspect but enough to spook the shit out of the suspect next to me so bad that he looked like he was about to hyperventilate. He fiddled around with his thumbs, cigarette packs and got jumpy every time I turned my head to look behind me. After over 40 minutes of standing next to me figuring out what the hell he was going to do he went up stairs and few minutes later he came down followed by another suspect pointing me out from the other side of the bar. They made the connection so obvious who they were it was hard not to ignore it.

The bottom line was that based on their history they were in the U.S for something really big but at that time, it was impossible to know exactly what, until 911 happened.

As far as I believe, the Special Agent I was in direct contact with and his closest supervisors were very serious about following up on these suspects that clearly coincided with the FBI note used as U.S. vs. Zacarias Moussaoui exhibit 792, but could not follow up due to the reluctance of those in charge in Washington or the main Radical Islamic Unit in New York to give them the green light to pursue these suspects. Given the little information and attention from Atta and Shehhi's presence in Atlanta, they were apparently obstructed from pursuing them as well. These decisions would have been critical in preventing 911 all together. As the 911 commission stated there were vast communication gaps and "the wall" between agencies hindered investigations from taking form. A lame excuse to say the least! Corruption and mismanagement played more of a significant part in the obstruction of any clear investigation in preventing terrorist plots and even investigations when terrorist plots had been discovered. Most often the only outcome is career protectionism to cover up mishaps such as with the negligence related to missed opportunities to prevent 911 and including missing or obstructing the opportunity to investigate or apprehend the Chechens within the report.

These minimum steps should have been conducted immediately upon receiving my reports;

- FBI agents or law enforcement should have had the flexibility to follow up with all witnesses including the staff at nightclub to take statements and provided that the nightclub was cooperative and or cleared with a search warrant to gather photos from surveillance cameras of suspects and any other evidence from possible witnesses. Other witnesses outside of the nightclub which already worked together with law enforcement were available at request.

- Should have secured the Russian nuclear engineer and his family until it was clear that no danger was present.

Given the nightclub staff's positive willingness to cooperate with me they would certainly have cooperated with investigators from law enforcement. They hardly needed reminders of the bombings at a gay club in Atlanta a couple of years earlier.[127]
While I worked with security at a 5 star hotel, I worked on some very basic security preparations for a gynecology conference. Because I noticed one of the topics of this conference was about abortion procedures I ran some risk assessment research of the attending guests. When asking management if this conference needed more than the regular security, the management thought that day to day security functions were enough. After all, an abortion clinic in Atlanta had been bombed by lone terrorists inspired by a Christian anti-abortion extremist group called Army of God (AOG) a few months earlier. This conference was no secret either. Information was openly available on the internet. Anyone that wanted to find out could run a search on internet search engines and they would get time and location. AOG seemed well informed given their claims of terrorist acts. My risk assessment research paid off despite being told not to. A VIP doctor that was scheduled to attend the seminar at the hotel owned

---

[127] "*ARMY OF GOD*" CLAIMS RESPONSIBILITY FOR *ATLANTA BOMBINGS;* Reuters News Agency, 1997 - FEB - 24; Associated Press, 1997 - FEB - 26

a clinic in Florida that has had a long history of being victimized by anti abortionists and even this particular group AOG. This doctor's spouse had in fact been gunned down and murdered and her clinic targeted numerous times for several years.[128] The doctor had repeatedly received threats to her life for years. With an extremist group still on the loose that had bombed two locations including an abortion clinic in Atlanta, her attendance was a very serious issue that required tighter security measures due to the fact that she faced threats by terrorists that had a history of carrying out assassinations and bombings. The conference planners and management at the hotel had no idea of the severity of the situation. They became alarmed only when I forced them to listen in private and described this doctor's history, the assassination of her husband, the threats she had received and added that the same group that claimed responsibility for the bombings in Atlanta also had threatened this doctor in the past. Then they woke up when I flashed the reality of bomb images in Atlanta. We were far from prepared to deal with that. Local law enforcement had not been notified prior to this situation. This was a situation where we would have needed law enforcement to standby or at least notified. I made the decision to talk with my friend who was the lead inspector of the criminal investigations division of the APD. I had coordinated other security issues with him involving major

---

[128] NARAL Pro-Choice America Foundation. (2006) Clinic violence and intimidation. Retrieved April 13, 2006.

VIP's and heads of State in the past. We eventually became good friends too. He is the contact that invited me to join their Criminal Information Network that was comprised of local, state, federal and private security specialists that reviewed trends and threats including terrorism. The doctor and abortion clinic owner canceled her trip as a result of the immediate high risk situation and little time to prepare for reasonable and appropriate security measures.

February 1997, an improvised explosive device (IED) exploded inside the Otherside Lounge, a gay club in the suburbs of Atlanta, injuring five.[129] A secondary IED had been placed outside to target responders and law enforcement. No one was injured by the second blast. This was the second incident where secondary bomb devices were used. An abortion clinic in Atlanta was the first to get hit. They too had been subjected to a secondary device. Army of God (AOG) claimed responsibility as with a number of abortion clinics their followers have targeted in the past.[130] Army of God was known to law enforcement as a mystical Christian anti abortion "group." Speculation by experts would argue whether they were a group at all. From my own research, Army of Gods recruitment methods were primarily done by selecting specific individuals who were distinctively aggressive and

[129] Officials Link Atlanta Bombings and Ask for Help By KEVIN SACK Published: Tuesday, June 10, 1997

[130] Anti-Abortion Extremists 'Patriots' and racists converge *By Frederick Clarkson Intelligence Report* Summer 1998 Southern Poverty Law Center

passionate at anti abortion protest rallies. Their selections of potential "loner terrorists" would receive anonymous mail in form of anti abortion, extreme rightwing Christian literature and terrorist "how to" manuals such as bomb making recipes by internet, mail and other mediators. Their materials were a catalyst inspiring a drive for hate against doctors who performed abortion. Anti abortion rallies usually had vast selections of extreme Christian Diasporas and passionately idealistic aggressive individuals to choose from. The Army of God could project an anonymous group of terrorist volunteers without displaying or exposing themselves. Despite AOG's efforts, volunteers or recruits were very limited but enough for a few to cause fear and terror among abortion clinics and their communities throughout the country especially along the east coast.

This same tactic is just as valid in jihadist recruiting processes of suicide bombers in Africa, Asia, Europe, Mideast and U.S. Internet and propaganda projects the impetus for volunteers.

Knowing that the staff at the nightclub had identified Interpol suspects in their club with a nasty history of hostage taking, the nightclub staff certainly had legitimate concerns with protecting both staff and their customers or guests. But who the hell is going to argue and order a major Interpol wanted terrorist identified in their nightclub to leave their premises. Given Basaev's history and statements to Paul there was no telling what he would do if provoked. All in all, the nightclub's staff and security did an excellent job and deed in their role!

For the FBI field agents, the limitations they were subjected to with hands tied behind their backs made any investigative approach counterproductive.

For a person like Shamil Basaev to walk around unsuspected in Atlanta, Georgia was literally surrealistic. But many up close and personal witnesses and I, standing no more than two feet face to face with short and long conversation with the suspects, left no doubt.

FBI in Phoenix and Minnesota blew the whistle on suspects that would later turn out that they were affiliated to the same Chechens from my report in Atlanta.

As far as the memos by the FBI in Phoenix, Minnesota, Paris and London Legat (Legal Attaches) and French authorities, Zacarias Moussaoui and Zacaria Soubra were transient members under Hizb uhr Tahrir and Al Muhajiroun and co-operative under Islamic Army of the Caucasus lead by Shamil Basaev and Ibn al Khattab.

Furthermore, it was alleged that most of the 9/11 hijackers had fought in or were on their way to fight under Shamil Basaev and Ibn al Khattab in Chechnya. [131]

---

[131] History Commons Timeline; Various articles sources regarding testimonies and sources concerning 911 hijackers fighting or plans to fight for Chechen mujahideen; .[Observer, 9/23/01 , ABC News, 1/9/02]

According to Congressional Testimony Inquiry, 7/24/03, CIA Director George Tenet; Khalid Almihdhar, Nawaf Alhazmi and Salem Alhazmi all fought in Chechnya. Khalid Almihdhar's family claims he fought in Chechnya in 1997 while the Alhazmi brothers fought in Chechnya in 1998. [Observer, 9/23/01, ABC News, 1/9/02], [Congressional Inquiry, 7/24/03, CIA Director Tenet Testimony, 6/18/02] [Los Angeles Times, 9/1/02] Ahmed Alhaznawi left for Chechnya in 1999 and Hamza, Ahmed's brother, went to Chechnya around January 2001 and apparently called home around June 2001 confirming that he was in Chechnya. Mohand Alshehri: went to fight in Chechnya in early 2000. [ABC News, 1/9/02], [Arab News, 9/22/01], [Independent, 9/27/01], [Washington Post, 9/25/01], [Arab News, 9/18/01] and [Arab News, 9/22/01]

 Ahmed Alghamdi dropped school and went on to fight in Chechnya in 2000, last seen by his family in December 2000. He last called his parents in July 2001 but didn't mention being in the U.S. [Arab News, 9/18/01, Arab News, 9/22/01]

These 911 hijackers that fought in Chechnya were clearly under orders and instructions by Shamil Basaev and Ibn al Khattab during the 911 planning stages and the execution of 911 which technically made them co-conspirators of 911. Another important fact about Shamil Basaev and Ibn al Khattab was that they were hands on leaders and always at front together with their men. This also means that Basaev himself would not be directing his men halfway around the world when they took part in the operations of 911. He would simply not allow his men to go 'behind enemy lines' without being there himself.

Four of the hijackers had strong desires and plans of fighting in Chechnya.

1. Members of the Hamburg cell Mohammed Atta, Marwan Alshehhi, Ziad Jarrah, and would-be hijacker Ramzi Bin al-Shibh wanted to fight in Chechnya but were told in early 2000 that they were needed elsewhere. [Washington Post, 10/23/2002; Reuters, 10/29/2002]

Mounir Mottasadeq, a Moroccan who was arrested among the Hamburg cell, was suspected of assisting 911 hijackers Atta, Alshehhi, Jarrah and al-Shibh acted as the Chechen cause liaison.

2. Waleed and Wail Alshehri in December 2000, spoke of fighting in Chechnya. Wail Alshehri had psychological problems, went with his brother to Mecca to seek help and both disappeared. [Washington Post, 9/25/01 , Arab News, 9/18/01]

3. Ahmed Alnami who had left home in June 2000 had pledged Jihad together with Alshehri brothers and Ahmed Alghamdi, who took part in fighting in Chechnya. [Arab News, 9/19/01 , Washington Post, 9/25/01] However, the only distinction of his alleged intentions to fight in Chechnya was the pledge.

4. Fayez Ahmed Banihammad: left home in July 2000 saying he wanted to participate in a holy war or do relief work. [St.

Petersburg Times, 9/27/01 , Washington Post, 9/25/01] He called his parents one time since. [Arab News, 9/18/01]

5. Majed Moqed: Trained by Louai al Sakka together with al Suqami and four others in Turkey for fighting in Chechnya. Moqed spent time with Hamburg cells Chechen liaison Hani Hanjour in New Jersey.

The fact that most of the 911 hijackers had fought or intended to fight in Chechnya under Ibn al Khattab and Shamil Basaev, it was highly likely that they would have responded to orders from Ibn al Khattab as candidates for 911. Ibn al Khattab and Basaev also seemed to have tactical and on hands and transnational experience with leading operations like 911. 911 was a long planned but still low cost operational campaign that hit several vulnerable points with multi hijackings under one operation. This had all the hallmarks of the type of tactical planning Ibn al Khattab and Shamil Basaev had previous experience with. Basaev had several successes hijacking airliners making them well suited to play an important role in the planning and execution of 911 alongside al Qaida. Campaigns like Budenovsk and Beslan were done with inside help from corrupt Russians. Basaev and Khattab were connected to either side riddled with ties to a combination of corrupted GRU officers and CIA collaborations with Turks and Saudis through Noukhaev, Saidov and Surikov.

Hawk of Pandora

The west and especially the Bush administration had hushed most
of Chechens connections to 911.[132] Apart from oil investments in
the Caucasus around the Caspian Sea, the Neocons had too many
close connections related to involvements in Turkey and
Chechnya. It would be the new Mujahideen frontier against
Russia supporting and breeding a new line of terrorists for the
future. Like the Iran Contra scandal deals involving cocaine from
Columbia to support arms for the Contra's and trading arms for
hostages in Iran. The same network of players from Iran/Contra
through Bank of Credit and Commerce International (BCCI) were
at it again, this time dealing with arms for heroin from
Afghanistan through the Caucasus and Turkey while sponsoring
the Chechen Mujahideen.

Founders and members of both, the American Turkish Council
(ATC) and American Committee for Peace in Chechnya (ACPC),
Richard Perle and Stephen Solarz were well connected to Turkish
intelligence. Khoz Noukhaev, Anton Surikov and Ruslan Saidov
were perfect- plausibly deniable- liaisons that provided covert
support to the Chechens contracted on behalf of Anton Surikov's
associations to either Halliburton or former CIA officer, Fritz
Ermarth with the backing of Perle, Solarz and other members of
ATC and ACPC. Anton Surikov has openly admitted to his
associations to Fritz Ermarth.[133] Ruslan Saidov's positions as

---

[132] Reuters has reported: "Western diplomats play down any Chechen involvement by al-Qaeda." [Reuters, 10/24/02]
[133] Yasenev's allegations that "Surikov has contacts with F. Ermarth," Surikov r esponded: "I am personallyacquainted with Mr. Ermarth as political scientist si

intelligence officer for both Chechen and Turkish intelligence provided Turkey with unofficially sponsored support for Chechens, due to generations of close ethnic loyalty. Another was Ruslan Saidov's close ties to the Wahhab community in Turkey. Ruslan Saidov's close friendship to Ibn al Khattab defines his mediation between Turkey, the Chechens and Al Qaida. This concurs with former FBI translator Sibel Edmonds' reactions of an article about a self confessed and convicted high ranking al Qaida member originally from Syria who trained several 911 terrorists to prepare for fighting in Chechnya under Ibn al Khattab.

Louai al Sakka, who is serving a prison sentence in Turkey for supporting terrorist activities related to 911 on behalf of "Al Qaida", initially trained Mujahideen for Chechnya.[134] The six 911 hijackers that had been trained by al Sakka were Ahmed, Hamza and Saeed al Ghamdi, Nawaf al-Hazmi, Majed Moqed and Satam al-Suqami, four of them were intended to join Ibn al Khattab and Shamil Basaev's Islamic Army of the Caucasus but were unable to cross the south Georgian border. The two others were to move on to Afghanistan.

---

nce 1996. It's wellknown by many people and we never hid this fact." Email between Anton Surikov and Oleg Grechenevsky 09/17/05 http://www.mail-archive.com/cia-drugs@yahoogroups.com/msg01967.html Original source; Cf. *Argumenty i Facty*, 9/15/99, http://www.aif.ru/oldsite/986/art010.html.

[134] Al - Qaeda kingpin: I trained 9/11 hijackers
Chris Gourlay and Jonathan Calvert The Sunday Times November 25, 2007

Hawk of Pandora

The ATC members or "high value" suspects under FBI investigation for aiding and profiting from arms and drug (heroin) trafficking, based on Sibel Edmonds' translated documents witnessing the growing evidence, obviously had central interests in the trafficking pipelines from the "Stan's" being Afghanistan, Pakistan, Uzbekistan, Kazakhstan, Kirgizstan and Tajikistan provided by Noukhaev and Saidov's channels. Louai al Sakka's involvement was a serious conflict of interest and another reason why Ashcroft imposed the states secrets privilege on Sibel Edmonds to keep her from testifying about the documents she translated for the FBI investigation on ATC members. If Americans and the rest of the world had jury voice regarding Sibel Edmonds' genuine testimonies regarding the illicit activities of Perle, Feith, Grossman, Edelman, Solarz and other suspects in her "State Secrets Privilege Gallery", these individuals would have been indicted for high treason and charges of sponsoring terrorism and rogue nations with the means of developing nuclear capabilities. ATC high value suspects were obvious catalysts obstructing investigations that could have prevented 911. Ashcroft obviously had conflicts of interest with the translated evidence for several reasons. He was closely associated to the high value suspects. Richard Perle's positions as CEO for Trireme Partners, board member for Autonomy Corp and advisor for Global Crossing had government contracts with Dept of Justice, Dept of Defense and Homeland Security for surveillance programs which

Attorney General John Ashcroft approved in 2001.[135] Autonomy and Global Crossing provided surveillance technology for DoD, NSA and FBI's new data mining system.[136] [137]

"In 2003, the company signed a precedent-setting Network Security Agreement with the Departments of Homeland Security, Defense and Justice and the Federal Bureau of Investigation to support law enforcement and national security objectives." Global Crossing's web http://www.globalcrossing.com/news/2005/october/10.aspx.

Trireme Partners provided similar technological services. Richard Perle has an extensive reputation to influence and advocate murky and corrupt conditions with companies and countries he did business with. This is among the reasons why he was knick named Prince of Darkness in Washington by friends and foes. My ADSL service provider used Global Crossing's fiber optic technology when my computer was being data mined in June 2003.

Another former GRU officer contracted by Halliburton subsidiary KBR known as the "Merchant of Death," Victor Bout also had

---

[135] Justice Department Probe Foiled By Shane Harris and Murray Waas, *National Journal*
Thursday, May 25, 2006
[136] http://www.autonomy.com/content/News/Releases/2007/0625a.en.html
[137] http://www.globalcrossing.com/news/2005/october/10.aspx

extensive ties to Al Qaida.[138] Victor Bout was arrested in
Thailand march 2008 and indicted by US attorney's office for
providing arms to the Colombian terrorist organization FARC
(Bout's arms sales to Al Qaida and Taliban were not mentioned in
the indictment) was another added to the long list of arms
trafficking associates linked to the Bush administrations cronies.
Viktor Bout had been hired by Halliburton for air transport
contracts to fly "supplies" into Baghdad international airport on
American taxpayers bills.[139] This demonstrates Cheney's corrupt
double standard nature as the former CEO of Halliburton right
before he took office as vice president. And that Halliburton had
gained some of the highest no bid contracts after 911. Halliburton
and its subsidiary Kellogg, Brown and Root (KBR) had been
under fire for several cases of fraud and overcharging their
services to the military. Cheney had clear influence over
Halliburton without taking any steps to stop their abuses and
criminal acts.

"Halliburton billed the government for 42,000 meals a day for our
troops, but only served 14,000 meals a day. Halliburton charged
the government $45 for cases of locally produced soda and $100
to wash a few bags of laundry. Halliburton paid local citizens 50
cents an hour for laundry work. Examination of seven fully paid
Halliburton LOGCAP task orders with a combined value of $4.33

---

[138] "Ring, Possible Links with Taliban," *Le Soir* [Brussels], 9 February 2002.
<http://www.nisat.org>

billion identified unsupported costs totaling $1.82 billion. Nearly half of every dollar spent (42 cents) could not be justified."[140]

KBR also came under fire ordering their own men to run unarmored and unarmed supply convoys which resulted in their deaths by terrorists which Victor Bout was known to have supplied weapons to. Their partner companies BAE's subsidiary Armor Holding Inc. provided faulty armor to the military. According to Project on Government Oversight's Federal Contract Misconduct Database, Halliburton, KBR, Armor Holdings and several other wartime contractors have been charged with over 40 fraud, kickback, overcharging and corruption cases since the Iraq war.[141] Yet while they complained that the military could not adequately protect the airport due to lack of support, they hired a dirty arms merchant with a long and documented history of selling weapons to terrorist groups including Al Qaida and Taliban. Even though Viktor Bout provided alternative air transport and shipments, he seemed to have free passes wherever he went despite international warrants against him for breaching arms embargoes. Then National Security Advisor Condoleezza Rice insured the free passes by ordering National Security Council investigators to stay away

---

[139] Judy Pasternak and Stephen Braun, "Following the Trail of Arms to Al-Qaida," *Los Angeles Times*, 21 January 2002. <http://www.nisat.org>

[140] Halliburton cases of Corruption, http://www.halliburtonwatch.org/about_hal/about.html

[141] Project on Government Oversight Federal Contract Misconduct Database http://www.contractormisconduct.org/

from Victor Bout.[142] They could observe but not investigate. When the heat turned to the government contractor (KBR/Halliburton) came too close as a result of high level protests after a few articles connecting Bout's private contracts linking the Bush and Cheney administration, it was time to get rid of his services and he was finally arrested by the Thai authorities at the request of the U.S Justice Department/Drug Enforcement Administration (DEA).

Cheney, the former CEO of Halliburton, is adamant that anyone who supports or sponsors terrorism is guilty of terrorism. He was also unwavering about using torture and water boarding against terrorists, yet his former company that he still supports and has a close relationship to is under his own definition a sponsor of terrorism. His Neocon staff was also equally engaged with conducting business with sponsors of terrorism such as; their close relationship to Adnan Khashoggi, a close associate to bin Laden, Neil Bush business interests with Boris Berezovsky. Berezovsky provided millions of dollars to Shamil Basaev and Osama bin Laden's second Lieutenant Ibn al Khattab. That must mean (under Cheney's own definitions of support) they too were equally qualified as "suspects" who should have resided at Guantanamo, Cuba, with torture and water boarding included.

---

[142] Arms and the Man By PETER LANDESMAN Published: Sunday, August 17, 2003 New York Times Magazine

If Cheney was so unwavering about protecting the US against terrorism and defending torture, why didn't he do something to charge or freeze Halliburton's assets? From 2001 to 2005, Cheney was still getting paid by Halliburton for "deferred salary payments" way above the amount he earned as Vice President and also owns major stockholder options which skyrocketed during Halliburton's war profits.[143] This obviously means that the more Cheney can support terrorists and market fear of terrorism or even sanction false flag terrorist incidents the more money he stands to gain. Hundreds of millions of dollars is hell of a motive! The conditions for profiting by terrorism are obviously offered by collaborating and conducting business with people providing arms to, training and supporting terrorists. These hierarchical liaisons of the Caucasus criminal world sustain the nexus between terrorism and its support by drug trafficking connections between central Asia, the Caucasus, Balkans and Europe.

It has also been well documented that these terrorist groups are intertwined with organized crime activities such as arms and drug trafficking (which supplies European and US narcotic markets).[144] According to a federal research report by the Federal Research Division in partnership with DoD; Al Qaida, Islamic Army of the

---

[143] Dick Cheney Rules June 3, 2007 EDITORIAL New York Times
[144] A GLOBAL OVERVIEW OF NARCOTICS-FUNDED TERRORIST AND OTHER EXTREMIST GROUPS; *A Report Prepared by the Federal Research Division, Library of Congress under an Interagency Agreement with the Department of Defense May 2002* Researchers: LaVerle Berry, Glenn E. Curtis, Rex A. Hudson and Nina A. K. Project Manager: Rex A. Hudson

Caucasus (Chechnya, Dagestan and Abkhazia), Islamic
Movement of Uzbekistan (Uzbekistan, Tajikstan) and Hizb ut
Tahrir (Palestine, Lebanon, Caucasus and Central Asia),
Hezbollah (Iran, Lebanon, Syria and Turkey), Popular Front for
Liberation of Palestine- General Command (Palestine, Lebanon
and Syria) and FARC (Columbia) all have partially financed their
terrorist organizations and activities from narcotics trafficking. [145]

- Al Qaida and Taliban took profit taxes from poppy farmers in
  Afghanistan. Heroin trafficking is a major source of income.
- Kosovo Liberation Army (KLA); Apart from major support
  by the west. KLA's main funding came from Heroin
  trafficking mainly from Afghanistan through Turkey.
- The Islamic Movement of Uzbekistan (IMU) gains much of
  its funding from narcotics trafficking through Central Asian
  routes to support its military, political, and propaganda
  activities. That trafficking is based on moving heroin from
  Afghanistan
  through Tajikistan, Uzbekistan, and Kyrgyzstan, into Russia,
  and then into Western Europe.
- Hizb Uhr Tahrir receives most support from outside
  organizational support but oversees protection of heroin
  shipments through their territories in Uzbekistan and
  Tajikistan.

---

[145] Ibid

- Islamic Army of the Caucasus led by (late) Shamil Basaev gained substantial sources of income through protection for support from the organized crime community "Obshina" formerly run by Khoz Noukhaev, Gelaev and Arbi Baraev's gang controlling trafficking routes through the Caucasus regions in Georgia and Russia. Arbi Baraev mainly controlled trafficking through the Pankisi Gorge through to Abkhazia. Much of this went on through Turkey or Ukraine.
- Hezbollah earned income through trafficking heroin and providing protection on trafficking routes from Iran, Lebanon, Syria and Turkey to South America.
- PFLP-GC also earned income from various criminal activities involving heroin trafficking.
- FARC earns income through cocaine production and trafficking and protection to other cartels.

Everyone who traffics with intent to distribute or use cocaine and heroin are inherently sponsors in supplying the cycle between corruption, crime and terrorism.

The al Qaida transpired groups connect Islamic terrorist proxies from Afghanistan to the Caucasus via Islamic Movement of Uzbekistan (IMU) and Hizb uhr Tahrir (HUT) that transports or protects heroin shipments through their territories to Russia (Caucasus) or Turkey and then to Europe also known as the "Silk Road" and the "Balkan Route" in exchange for arms. Afghanistan is the source country that provides 90% of all opium made into heroin worldwide. The FBI's investigation into ATC high value targets was based on, among other allegations, whether sources of profits from their lobbying activities originated from drug trafficking proceeds. They were also investigated for leaking information on U.S investigations through middlemen (among plausible suspects, Anton Surikov and Ruslan Saidov that were close to the Turkish and Uzbekistan intelligence community) to IMU, HUT, the Chechens, Khoz Noukhaev and KLA, making them high value lobbying assets of the underworld. A key fact is that it is impossible to conduct business without dealing with highly corrupt officials in Central Asian countries or regions in the Caucasus. Political corruption in the Caucasus and Central Asian countries is alpha and omega with the groups involved with organized crime and terrorism. One can easily estimate that there is a 99% certainty that their (ATC's) business interests in these countries involved corrupt officials linked to organized crime members and terrorist groups. Therefore profits they received most likely originated from these criminal sources.

Douglas Feith and Richard Perle's company, International Advisors Inc. (IAI), formed in 1989 and registered as a Turkish Foreign Agent with the Justice Department,[146] were also influential in convincing the Turkish government to train and arm Albanian (KLA) and Bosnian Muslims. Perle also cosigned a Project for New American Century (PNAC), a letter to President

---

[146] Profiles; Douglas Feith and Richard Perle. Rightweb.org

Clinton urging him to support Albanians (i.e KLA).[147] It was not long after that the KLA who was taken off the State Dept's list of terrorist groups that intelligence reports from International law enforcement, Interpol, DEA and other U.S federal law enforcement and intelligence agencies began surfacing that KLA had become a major player of the heroin trafficking market. Most of the heroin shipments were trafficked through Turkey. Therefore ATC high value suspects' activities were defined with reasonable suspicion of criminal negligence far beyond any coincidental factors.

With all of their (illegitimate) investments in the Caucasus and Central Asia any kind of favorable connections to groups from the Caucasus to Kazakhstan connected to Al Qaida would certainly risk public outcry and any investments already in place. Chechens were certainly among them. In many cases already has caused some public protests but not nearly enough.

There are too many patterns that relay many of the members of the Bush administration, their committees along with Democrats endorsing and sponsoring terrorist groups behind the curtains that are closely tied to Al Qaida that it is amazing how people could support them or any other administration that adheres to similar policies. The patriotic value to vote republican or democrat is the

[147] Letter to President Clinton regarding support for Kosovo, Project for New American Century.
http://www.newamericancentury.org/kosovomilosevicsep98.htm

peer pressure that secures the powers of these parties to cover up for corrupt policies.

It is not a shock to understand that many within the Bush and Cheney administration and their corporate alliance benefitted enormously from 911 and the wars that followed despite the catastrophic consequences for Americans and the world.

What was not surprising was the deliberate ignorance and refusal to acknowledge all the red warnings that came forth prior to 911.

The Red Warnings

'Neglect of facing social problems or taking responsibility for these problems entraps everyone involved. Therefore, fear of formidable choices results in resisting any form of temptation to justify reasonable acts of conscious.' Author

From the end of the 90's there was literally an abundance of pre 911 warnings. Warnings came all across the world from Asia, Europe and the Middle East. Over ten countries warned of a potential attack. Many overlapping and collaborating warnings predicting the same type of attack! Terrorists would use planes. Most of these warnings clearly pointed to al Qaida and affiliated groups as the source of the threat.

There were several major warnings in regards to Chechens involvement with 911 and their links to al Qaida that clearly coincided with the report faxed to the FBI field office in Atlanta Dec 30, 2000.

Both the CIA and FBI had prior knowledge of relevant warnings and events related to the Chechens involvement with 911;

On the morning of July 10, 2001 CIA Director (DCI) George Tenet received an urgent intelligence briefing from counterterrorism chief Cofer Black concerning a range of warnings of a "significant attack" from different intelligence sources.

One of the warnings related to Chechen mujahedeen leader Ibn al Khattab (Shamil Basaev's close partner) indicating that a terrorist attack would soon happen; Khattab had promised some "very big news" to his fighters. This communication was apparently passed on to the CIA.

DCI George Tenet found the briefing urgent enough to call then National Security Adviser Condoleezza Rice for an extra meeting attended by Cofer Black, Richard Blee (CIA's Bin Laden unit chief), Stephen Hadley (Deputy National Security Adviser) and Richard Clark (Counterterrorism "tzar"). *[McClatchy Newspapers, 10/2/2006]*

According to author Bob Woodward in his book "Plan of Attack", Condoleezza Rice had brushed off Tenet and Blacks urgent warning. "Tenet and Black will both later recall the meeting as the starkest warning they gave the White House on al-Qaeda before 9/11 and one that could have potentially stopped the 9/11 attacks if Rice had acted on it and conveyed their urgency to President Bush." *[Woodward, 2006, pp. 80]*

As early as 1999, French intelligence accumulated information from numerous investigations regarding Al Qaida, Chechen and Russian activities.

A significant intelligence event that coincided with French intelligence warnings to both the FBI and CIA, according to Versiya and Le Monde, was an apparent meeting that occurred in the south of France, at the villa of Adnan Khashoggi July, 1999,

noted in reports by distinguished scholars like professors John B
Dunlop's "Storm in Moscow": A Plan of the Yeltsin "Family" to
Destabilize Russia, The Hoover Institution, October 8, 2004 and
Peter Dale Scott's The Global Drug Meta-Group: Drugs,
Managed Violence, and the Russian 9/11. [148]

Despite contrary allegations regarding the meeting at Adnan
Khashoggi's villa in southern France, Anton Surikov, the meeting
planner, clarifies in his email correspondence with Oleg
Grechenevsky that Kagarlitsky's Novaya Gazeta article on the
meeting in France was not directed by him. Anton Surikov still
confirms more than he denies. Surikov denies, in the emails,
being the primary source of Kagarlitsky's article but provided
details for his article. Surikov never denies the meeting's
existence. [149] [150] Instead of stating straight out that the meeting
never takes place, he hints that the information regarding the
meeting at Khashoggi's villa has partial inaccuracies. Versiya
(lacked documented evidence), Novaya Gazeta, Stringer and Le
Monde all wrote similar articles of meeting or activities at
Khashoggi's villa citing separate sources.

---

[148] "Storm in Moscow": A Plan of the Yeltsin "Family" to Destabilize Russia
John B. Dunlop The Hoover Institution October 8, 2004 and The Global Drug
Meta-Group: Drugs, Managed Violence, and the Russian 9/11 By Peter Dale
Scott

[149] Email between Anton Surikov and Oleg Grechenevsky 09/17/05
http://www.mail-archive.com/cia-drugs@yahoogroups.com/msg01967.html
original source from Cf. *Argumenty i Facty*, 9/15/99,
http://www.aif.ru/oldsite/986/art010.html.

[150] Interview, http://www.pravda.info/region/3601.html, discussed below. Cf.
Letter of Anton Surikov to Oleg Grechenevsky,

Also late KGB agent Alexander Litvinenko has distinguished the information worthy of mentioning in his reports and books.[151] Alexander Litvinenko is the former KGB and FSB agent that died of acute cancer as a result of direct contact with the radioactive substance Polonium. British officials and western media regarded the Litvinenko case as murder. British government convened with investigations alleging that the FSB loyal to Vladimir Putin were behind the assassination.

Although the KGB is known for assassinating their targets with poisons such as the use of Ricin, the murder by Polonium story seems somewhat vague. Transporting a highly radioactive substance like pure Polonium (Po-210) is extremely difficult and dangerous without adequate containment, which falls under strict international transportation regulations of hazardous materials. However, in small quantities Polonium is very difficult to detect during transportation if adequately contained. It is also allegedly very difficult to detect if ingested. Nevertheless, smuggling small quantities of pure Polonium, as indicated in the Litvinenko case, with poor containment or opened; traces will be left anywhere the bearer takes it as the Litvinenko case has shown. Traces were found on flights from Moscow to London, at a soccer stadium, hotels in London, Sushi bar where Litvinenko was allegedly

---

[151] "Blowing up Russian" by Alexander Litvinenko and Vladimir Feltshinsky 2006 (Following the books second edition released 2006, p 65. Litvinenko was exposed to polonium a highly radioactive material. Litvinenko died but a criminal investigation is still current alleging that Litvinenko was deliberately poisoned by FSB agents or contract assassins.)

poisoned and many who came in contact with the individual that transported and was in contact with the Polonium. Litvinenko allegedly died due to internal consumption of Polonium from drinking tea that contained a very small quantity but highly concentrated radioactive dose of alpha particles. Litvinenko was the only individual exposed enough to the radioactive material to die from it. The traces left by Andrei Lugovoi and Dmitri Kovtun would suggests that he may have had it transported through Kovtun who is under investigation in Germany for smuggling Plutonium. Kovtun was the only other suspect allegedly hospitalized after being exposed to Polonium. It's plausible that enough particles emitted from the carrier (Kovtun) made its way into Litvinenko's tea which was enough to kill Litvinenko. Polonium omits Alpha radiation particles that can kill only if inhaled or ingested internally. Any unsafe transfer of a container with Polonium could easily omit enough alpha particles to kill a person as Litvinenko fatally experienced.

"One gram of Po^{210} could thus in theory poison 20 million people of whom 10 million would die. The actual toxicity of Po^{210} is lower than these estimates, because radiation exposure that is spread out over several weeks (the biological half-life of polonium in humans is 30 to 50 days) is somewhat less damaging than an instantaneous dose.[152] It has been estimated that a median

---

[152] "Effective half-life of polonium in the human"
http://www.osti.gov/energycitations/product.biblio.jsp?osti_id=7162390
Retrieved 2009-15-08

lethal dose of ^{210}Po is 0.015 GBq (0.4 mCi), or 0.089 micrograms, still an extremely small amount."[153]

It is likely that Polonium was intended for other means such as nuclear smuggling for nuclear terrorism due to its use as an element in detonators for nuclear weapons, and that since such small undetectable quantities have a capacity of killing mass amount of individuals.

While Litvinenko investigated the Russian apartment building bombings he eventually turned to Islam. Litvinenko was alleged to have supported the Chechen cause and was suspected of smuggling nuclear materials as far back as 2000.[154] Litvinenko's inner circles of associate, Italian security expert, Mario Scaramella, stated during questioning that Litvinenko told Scaramella of his nuclear smuggling activities. [155] Litvinenko's statement to Scaramella strongly indicates a careless transaction of Polonium between Luguvoi, Kovtun and Litvinenko at the Sushi bar where they were apparently poisoned.

Aleksander Litvinenko's case opened up new mysteries and stories, many of which didn't add up to official reports of the investigation. Despite no specific mention of Surikov's network being involved, there are considerable motives and patterns to

---

[153] "Polonium Poisoning"
http://nuclearweaponarchive.org/News/PoloniumPoison.html Retrieved 2009-15-08.
[154] "Litvinenko, Nuclear Arms Trafficking and Chechens" Wayne Madsen Report, Wayne Madsen, 2007.

Surikov and his associates being directly involved with both Russia's apartment building bombings and playing a hand in 911 in the US. The meeting in southern France supports the notion of how these villains plan events that spark wars.

As reported by Versiya, Russian military intelligence GRU Col Anton Surikov had arranged a mystical meeting at Adnan Khashoggi's villa where there were several shady individuals present.[156] Among those alleged to be present at this meeting was GRU (Russian Military Intelligence) col. Anton Surikov, Chechen field commander Shamil Basaev, Evgeny Primakov, close friend of Ibn al Khattab and Chechen Intelligence Col. Ugur Mehmed aka Ruslan Saidov and Abkhaz minister of defense Sosnialev. Others alleged to be present at the meeting were from Israel and Venezuela. Jacob Kozman, a Russian/Israeli businessman with a shady history and last but not least host and short term resident Alfonso Davidovich, another shady Venezuelan banker with alleged relationships to FARC and other insurgent groups.[157]

---

[155] Litvinenko 'smuggled nuclear material' By Cahal Milmo, Peter Popham and Jason Bennetto The Independent *Wednesday, 29 November 2006*
[156] John B. Dunlop, "Storm in Moscow": A Plan of the Yeltsin "Family" to Destabilize Russia; Original story of the Meeting at Khashoggi's villa in Southern France was printed by Versiya 1999. Other versions with separate sources printed by Le Monde and Stringer have been documented and reviewed in The Global Drug Meta-Group: Drugs, Managed Violence, and the Russian 9/11 By Peter Dale Scott. The meeting was also discussed in Alexander Litvinenko's book "Blowing Up Russia."
[157] The article "Rossiyu zhdet oranzhevaya revolytsiya," *compormat.ru*, 17 December 2004 reports that Davidovich lives in Munich and enjoys both German and Venezuelan citizenship. He is also said to be personally acquainted with international arms dealer Khashoggi.

Davidovich is responsible for Far West Ltd's office in Bogota, Colombia.

The meeting that occurred at the villa supposedly took place July 4, 1999, was primarily focused on the upcoming invasion of Dagestan. A few days later Chechen field commanders Shamil Basaev and Ibn al Khattab invaded Dagestan.[158]

French intelligence would have several reasons to be concerned following the supposed meeting with the prominent Chechen Field commander and other leaders from the Caucasus region in southern France. Several of these big shots had strong ties to al Qaida.

Another concern was the intelligence from their source in Uzbekistan apparently describing plans to hijack planes possibly from France or Germany.[159]

"In early 2000 in Kabul, Afghanistan, bin Laden met with Taliban leaders and members of armed groups from Chechnya and discussed the possibility of hijacking a plane that would take off from Frankfurt, Germany, the note said, citing Uzbek intelligence."

---

[158] Richard Sakwa, ed (2005). "Robert Bruce Ware: Mythology and Political Failure in Chechnya". *Chechnya: From Past to Future*. Anthem Press. pp. 79-115

[159] "September 11, 2001; How much the French knew." Le Monde (Paris) 15 April, 2007

The third was that among these hijackers was a French citizen born in Morocco involved with a group of individuals tied to a correlation of al Qaida and Chechen leaders. This French citizen was Zacarias Moussaoui.[160]

Zacarias Moussaoui was by many who investigated his arrest and the circumstances around his activities in the U.S a significant catch. Then attorney general John Ashcroft labeled Moussaoui for being the 20th hijacker.[161] As a result of the persistence of FBI field agents and the cooperation between FBI field offices in Phoenix, Minnesota and Immigration and Naturalization Services (INS) managed to arrest him August 16, 2001, before he was able to complete the terrorist mission he apparently set out to commit. Khaled Sheik Muhammed (KSM), the alleged mastermind behind 911, confessed by secondary testimony (cited confessions from water boarding and other torture techniques), that Zacarias Moussaoui was not initially among the original 911 conspiracy group but was probably a part of another or secondary operation.[162] KSM also testified on plans for surveillance of U.S. nuclear power plants in order to attack them. It is uncertain exactly who was to carry out these types of attacks, however, the

---

[160] Findlaw US vs Zacarias Moussaoui Defense Exhibits

[161] How the Moussaoui Case Crumbled By Viveca Novak In WASHINGTON Sunday, Oct. 19, 2003 Time

[162] CIA's Harsh Interrogation Techniques Described: Sources Say Agency's Tactics Lead to Questionable Confessions, Sometimes to Death, *ABC News*, November 18, 2005

Chechens in my report have a solid history of conducting the type of raids needed to attack a U.S nuclear power plant.[163]

It is reasonable to note that the secondary testimony should be considered with a pinch of salt due to the fact that Khaled's testimony was taken during the process of being tortured [water boarded]. Torture has been argued by many experts as useless in regards to achieving truthful confessions. The result would end in untruthful confessions in order to end the enormous pain endured by torture.[164]

By end of 2000, the short summary report called "Hijacking of an airplane by Radical Islamists" filed by French intelligence, depicted detailed conversations between bin Laden, Chechen leader Ibn al Khattab, and the Taliban about a hijacking against US airlines.[165]

Different conversations took place between early 2000 and October 2000 between Chechen leaders and Al Qaida.[166]

It was between October 14, 15 and November 6, 2000, that Shamil Basaev was spotted several places in Atlanta by several witnesses including colleagues of the public safety group, manager and staff at the nightclub and I. Following 6 others later identified from the same Interpol file on Shamil Basaev and several others that was with the group but was unable to initially

---

[163] Khalid Sheikh Mohammed's '31 plots', *BBC*, March 15, 2007
[164] Ibid
[165] La Repubblica
[166] Ibid

identify by either pictures or other documented sources. But one of these unknowns was relevant due to overhearing this suspect describing to a girl he "was from the Russian federation" and hinted north of the "Caspian sea." He introduced the girl to some of the suspects standing together. What made this conversation obvious was the guy's utter pride in where he was from. I was actually waiting for this guy to begin bragging about their terrorist successes and war stories. This is because Caucasians and especially Chechens are profoundly proud of their warrior background. That is their identity.

Report was sent twice in 2000. One to the public safety group commander on 20 Dec, 2000, and a full report with updates regarding 6 other suspects from the same Interpol warrant to the special agent in charge (SAC) with the counter terrorism task force FBI field office Atlanta, Georgia 30 December, 2000.

The so-called result of what high ranking intelligence and federal law enforcement agency officials call "the wall", information that correspond from separate sources is not shared among agencies working on criminal or counter terrorist investigations. While the FBI received their information on Zacarias Moussaoui from Legat (Legal Attaché US Embassy) in Paris and London with background information on Moussaoui from French law enforcement authorities, the intelligence related to the Uzbekistan information was according to the French intelligence forwarded to CIA. FBI and CIA have often been known to be reluctant in sharing detailed information or intelligence due to many conflicts of interests in investigations. The CIA often uses assets which FBI often investigates for criminal activities. The same problem is also prevalent in other countries.

The small information exchanges between the FBI and CIA did confirm Khattab's connection to Osama bin Laden.

Although the intelligence from Uzbekistan has been disputed, the French undoubtedly had interests in these issues because these involved French citizens and possible terrorist activities on French soil.[167]

France has had numerous experiences with terrorist groups' especially involving Algerian and Moroccan extremists committing acts of terrorism on behalf of Armed Islamic Group (GIA) with shared strongholds and bases out of Algeria and Northern Morocco.[168] A notable event in terrorist history in the homeland of France involving GIA was the double bombings in Paris targeting the subway system.[169]

On July 25, 1995, Algerian terrorists rigged a gas canister with nails that exploded inside the St. Michel rail station in Paris. The explosion killed seven and wounding more than 150 and amounted to the deadliest from GIA's bombing campaign in Paris. The second attack killed one and injured over 40.

---

[167] French Hijack Warning by Craig Murray April 19, 2007
[168] Patterns of Global terrorism, United States Department of State 2007
[169] Ibid

The French report continued, "The plot considers hijacking a US airliner flying from Frankfurt to the US or hijacking a French or German airliner. The French intelligence comes from Uzbek spies who have infiltrated the Islamic Movement of Uzbekistan (IMU), a militant group based in Uzbekistan next door to Afghanistan and closely tied to bin Laden and the Taliban. Some of the spies ended up in al-Qaeda training camps in Afghanistan. The French report makes clear that the information was independently verified from other sources, including satellite telephone intercepts and possibly spies recruited in France."[170] *Le Monde (Paris), 4/15/2007*

Regardless of what context the intelligence from France may have been perceived by U.S authorities, the value of many of the pre 911 warnings coinciding with the French warnings and the investigations by FBI in Minnesota and Phoenix left more than enough reasonable cause and conviction to cross examine all of these warnings, memos and reports.

Nonetheless, they missed out on the opportunity to cross examine these reports together before the attack of September 11, 2001. According to the FBI memo in the Moussaoui case, FBI field agents had arrested Zacarias Moussaoui just weeks before 911 on an extended visa violation despite the volume of discoveries that made him more interesting and regarded as a specific terrorist threat by the FBI. The information the French had on Zacarias supported warrants for further investigation but was blocked by

---

[170] Le Monde, Paris, 4/15/2007

superiors in Washington DC refusing to authorize the request for FISA (Foreign Intelligence Surveillance Act) warrants.

Colleen Rowley, the FBI Special Agent and Minneapolis Chief Division Counsel turned whistleblower, wrote a letter to FBI Director Mueller in protest of the lack of support or even allegations of deliberate mismanagement of pursuing a legal case against Moussaoui with his connections to Ibn al Khattab and Al Qaida. She writes in her Memo;[171]

"I feel that certain facts, including the following, have, up to now, been omitted, downplayed, glossed over and/or mis-characterized in an effort to avoid or minimize personal and/or institutional embarrassment on the part of the FBI and/or perhaps even for improper political reasons:

> **5)** The fact is that key FBIHQ personnel whose job it was to assist and coordinate with field division agents on terrorism investigations and the obtaining and use of FISA searches (and who theoretically were privy to many more sources of intelligence information than field division agents), continued to, almost inexplicably, throw up roadblocks and undermine Minneapolis' by-now desperate efforts to obtain a FISA search warrant, long after the French intelligence service provided its information and probable cause became clear.

---

[171] Coleen Rowley's Memo to FBI Director Robert Mueller, Time, May 21, 2002, http://www.time.com/time/covers/1101020603/memo.html

HQ personnel brought up almost ridiculous questions in their apparent efforts to undermine the probable cause.

In all of their conversations and correspondence, HQ personnel never disclosed to the Minneapolis agents that the Phoenix Division had, only approximately three weeks earlier, warned of Al Qaeda operatives in flight schools seeking flight training for terrorist purposes! "

Ashcroft told the 9/11 commission that FBI agents "sought approval for a criminal search warrant to search his computer. The warrant was rejected because FBI officials feared breaching the "wall." Actually, FBI agents in Minneapolis asked FBI headquarters for permission to request a search warrant from a federal judge in Minnesota.[172]

Already by April, 2001, FBI's Assistant Director of the counter terrorism division, Dale Watson, had already sent a memo to FBI Director Louis Freeh warning that Islamic radicals are planning a "terrorist operation." The memo states that "Sunni extremists with links to Ibn al Khattab, an extremist leader in Chechnya, and to Osama bin Laden [have been involved in] serious operational planning since late 2000, with an intended culmination in late spring 2001."[173] Watson says the planning was sparked by the renewal of the Palestinian Intifada in September 2000. "All the

---

[172] Ashcroft, 9/11, and Government as Victim by James Bovard The Future of Freedom Foundation; quoting 911 commission

[173] Federal Bureau of Investigation memo on the Chechens and Ibn al Khattab, 4/2001 US v Zacarias defense exhibit 792

players are heavily intertwined," the memo notes. Additionally, the memo says that "multiple sources also suggest that bin Laden's organization is planning a terrorist attack against US interests."

The Legat in London, much like the memo by the French, sent a memo regarding Zacarias Moussaoui during his residence in London while earning a master's degree from Cambridge and Southbank University and his approximate three week stay in London between flying in from Pakistan and then on to Chicago. It was in London that authorities believe he may have been recruited by Chechens named as "the Backstreet" cell and may have been assigned his operational duties in the US.

The descriptive intelligence on Zacarias Moussaoui by London Legat's sensitive source noted; [174]

MOUSSAOUI is an individual of superior intelligence who has a master's degree from Cambridge University. It was while residing in London that captioned subject "was taken in and initiated by the fundamentalists of "Backstreet" and Finsbury Park Mosque."

"MOUSSAOUI was a close associate of ███████, a Mujahideen who was killed in Chechnya in April 2000. ███████ like captioned subject was recruited and

---

[174] London Legal Attaché memo, Moussaoui's connections with Chechens in London. US v Zacarias defense exhibit

indoctrinated by the "Backstreet" and "Finsbury Park Group."

This apparently occurred in February 2001 while the group of Chechens was identified in Atlanta at "Nightclub" a couple of months earlier. The "Backstreet" and "Nightclub" group were the same group.

There was little doubt that Moussaoui had already been indoctrinated during his trips to Pakistan and his stay in London. Primarily there was little doubt about his affiliation to Chechen field commander Ibn al Khattab.

The Finsbury Park mosque has been a central part in recruiting fighters for the Mujahideen in Chechnya. Al Muhajiroun and Hizb uhr Tahrir were the groups providing recruitment and logistical support for Khattab and the Islamic Army of the Caucasus from North and South areas of England.

Ruslan Saidov, the "close friend" of Ibn Al Khattab and Shamil Basaev, had established connections with Hizb uhr Tahrir.

In 2003, Saidov, during a conference in Jordan hosted by Hizb uhr/ut Tahrir, Saidov conveyed that Hizb uhr Tahrir's presence in Russia had been an important development for the Mujahideen. Hizb uhr Tahrir has also sustained a presence in Central Asia and Crimea as well. Crimea is the peninsula on the Black sea that has sparked territorial disputes between Russia and Ukraine.[175]

---

[175] Shireen T. Hunter, *Islam in Russia: The Politics of Identity and Security* (Armonk, NY: M.E. Sharpe, 2004)

The FBI lawyers at HQ seemed hell bent on sticking to technicalities of refusing to issue FISA warrant on the basis that connecting Moussaoui as an "agent of a foreign power" for Khattab was insufficient. This didn't make any sense because of the fact that Khattab's role with Basaev as high ranking members of the mujahideen and political representatives in the Chechnyan republic actually did fit requirements for the FISA statute as 'agent of a foreign power'. Basaev and Khattab's famous invasion of Dagestan in 99' should have clearly qualified Khattab as a leader of a foreign power and Moussaoui as an agent representing Khattab as a leader of a foreign power. It is profoundly clear that the CIA and DoD were well aware of this since they had paid very close attention to all of the conflicts in the Caucasus and especially the Chechen wars. However, the CIA or DoD were restricted by law from interfering with Justice dept cases which was known as "the Wall".

FBI Minneapolis contacted CIA's Counter Terrorism Center (CTC) bypassing FBIHQ to get as much advance information on the Moussaoui/Khattab connection as possible. On August 14, 2001 the CIA had received their intelligence from Direction de la Surveillance du Territoire (DST) concerning a warning related to Moussaoui as a recruiter for Chechen leader Ibn al Khattab. The CIA's threat briefing August 30 and September 10, 2001 used as defense exhibits 672 and 674 in Moussaoui's trial acknowledged that Moussaoui was a recruiter for the Chechens.

Hawk of Pandora

For dumbfounded reasons lawyers at FBI headquarters turned down Minnesota agents' request for criminal search warrants of Moussaoui's computer. The same exact problem was obvious with FBI agents in Atlanta requesting search warrants for further evidence related to the Atlanta report 9 months earlier or even Atta's activities in Atlanta. In January, after speaking to the FBI agent I had sent the report to in Atlanta, he asked me to continue to follow up only in case the suspects happened to be sighted again. He was specific to convey not to approach or investigate them. That was clearly appropriate given the thin legal line of the whole situation. I and the few who covered my back when we discovered the other Chechens at the nightclub in November had absolutely no support or backing to continue to track their movements and report it. Had we taken any irrational engagements we would have been liable by law and none of us were interested in ending up in prison for taking more aggressive actions against these terrorist suspects which could have sparked a major violent incident with civilian casualties. By end of December, when these guys were nowhere to be found we were relieved although still concerned because I didn't have the support or jurisdiction which normally would have protected official field agents. At anytime I was an open target for the criminal networks that supported these Chechen suspects. Also another primary concern was "Why the FBI or local law enforcement did not take any feasible action to respond?" That kept dwelling through my mind the most despite the eagerness of my contact in the FBI field office. Why did they tie his hands and why transfer him in February when Atta was in town? The obstructions by the high ranking officials that surfaced after 911 shed light to that mystery. The FBI Phoenix office also had similar problems getting through to Washington headquarters and apparently received the same treatment of being hogtied at their field office. The well known Phoenix memo or "Williams memorandum" concerning suspects affiliated to the "Finsbury Park" cell in England was another angle from a suspect closely affiliated to Ibn al Khattab and the Chechens.

The Phoenix memo was titled "Zacarias Moustapha Soubra; IT - OTHER (Islamic Army of the Caucasus).

The Islamic Army of the Caucasus was the group lead by Shamil Basaev and Ibn al Khattab.

Zacaria Moustapha Soubra, born in Lebanon, gained focus by FBI's Phoenix office due to his involvement with Hizb Uhr Tahrir in England also known as Finsbury "group". It is important to mention that the Finsbury group originated as a result of the congested presence of Hizb uhr Tahrir and Muhajiroun which espoused a single Muslim state worldwide. Soubra was another 911 conspirator that had flown from England to the US. Although Soubra was only charged with visa or immigration violations he was never charged with terrorism charges. Perhaps he was just another "unwitting supporter" to the extremists involved with 911 or maybe other possible attacks. Nevertheless his association to

911 hijacker Hanjour that attended flight school in Arizona and given his representation to Hizb Uhr Tahrir who aided the group led by Basaev and Khattab it is likely that he was one of the connections to Zacarias Moussaoui in England.

Neither FBI offices in Minnesota or Phoenix received copies, to my knowledge, of my report which would have been a critical puzzle and generated more leads to Moussaoui's Chechen connection.

In light of the detailed report that the FBI were already in possession of regarding Chechens in Atlanta, the obstacles of the investigation into Moussaoui's connections with the Chechens in London were obvious obstructions by officials in Washington arguing that the agents in Minnesota needed proof connecting Chechens to a recognized terrorist group.

- *"FBI headquarters refused permission, instead insisting th at theMinnesota agents file a FISA search request which ha d to be handled by the experts at FBI headquarters.*

  Agents at FBI headquarters incorrectly insisted that FISA required Minneapolis agents to prove that Moussaoui was linked to a foreign power before a search warrant could be issued. Because a French intelligence agency indicated Moussaoui might be linked to the Chechen resistance, FBI headquarters insisted that Minneapolis agents find evidence connecting the Chechens to a recognized terrorist organization.

- *The congressional Joint Intelligence Committee report on pre9/11 failures noted that "because of this misunderstanding, Minneapolis [FBI agents] spent part of three weeks trying to connect the Chechen group to al Qaida." A 9/11 commission staff report concluded."[176]*

FBI Special Agent Greg Jones from the Minneapolis field office wrote in point one in his memo to FBIHQ, submitted as defense exhibit 349 in the indictment against Zacarias Moussaoui;

"1) I'm curious as to why the Al-Khattab/UBL info will be added later if it is what is required to establish the foreign power connection and therefore make the LHM fit the FISA requirements. It seems that we are setting this up for failure if we don't have the foreign power connection firmly established for the initial review."[177]

The 911 commission developed mostly by appointees of the Bush administration seemed persistent in avoiding the Chechen connection too. Knowing what kind of abuses the Bush and

---

[176] Ashcroft, 9/11, and Government as Victim by James Bovard; *author of* The Bush Betrayal *and* Terrorism & Tyranny: Trampling Freedom, Justice, and Peace to Rid the World of Evil *serves as a policy advisor for The Future of Freedom Foundation* quoting the 911 commission report.

[177] FBI Special Agent Memo to FBIHQ, U.S v Zacarias Moussaoui defense exhibit 349,

Cheney cabal was responsible for and looking back to the development of the 911 commission, it is reasonable to compare it with asking the devil to set up a commission to investigate evil. The 911 commission had concluded that the Chechen connection was a waste of Minnesota's field office efforts; it was obvious that they deliberately refused volumes of information proving quite the contrary. In actuality there were reports and information clearly confirming that Chechen field commander Ibn al Khattab and Shamil Basaev had close relationships with al Qaida and Osama bin Laden.

One of these [de]classified reports by Defense Intelligence Agency from 1998 that NGO organization Judicial Watch released in 2004 from a FOIA (Freedom of Information Act) request called "Swift Night" outlined descriptions of Ibn al Khattab as being a close friend and partner with Osama bin Laden (OBL).[178]

According to the Swift Night report, Khattab was a highly ranked member of al Qaida and organized training camps in Chechnya on behalf of OBL in 1995. By 1999, Khattab had made Chechnya his Jihad along with Shamil Basaev.

Other reports by United Nations had also indicated that Shamil Basaev himself had been trained at camps run by Osama bin Laden and al Qaida.[179]

---

[178] Judicial Watch FOIA request of Defense Intelligence agency 1998 declassified report released in 2004.
[179] "Chechen Mujahidin training at Al Qaida camps in Afghanistan" UN & Conflict Monitor United Nations Issue 9, Autumn 2000

Throughout most of the 911 investigation until the 911 commission released its report, the Chechen al Qaida connection was subjectively hushed down by government, the media and investigative branches.

The FBI Minnesota office had worked several weeks trying to obtain information and intelligence on a Chechen connection to a recognized terrorist organization despite the fact that the intelligence community knew that Chechen leader Khattab was a close associate to OBL. Again CIA had warned the White House that OBL and Khattab were planning 911 together. But the Chechen connection was without avail because until 2003 neither the US State department or other departments or agencies were willing to officially recognize Shamil Basaev and Ibn al Khattab as terrorist leaders connected to bin Laden and al Qaida despite reports from DIA, CIA, United Nations, Russian and Dagestan's Interpol warrants on them for terrorism, describing their affiliations and training with al Qaida.

The neoconservatives- both republicans and democrats- would have had many motives to hush down any obscure associations with shadowy Israeli, Pakistani and Turkish support for the Chechens. Due to 911 and Ibn al Khattab's close relationship with Osama bin Laden, not to mention several of the 911 hijackers, co-conspirator, Soubra and Moussaoui's close membership to the Al-Muhajiroun and Chechen group Islamic Army of the Caucasus led by Shamil Basaev and Ibn al Khattab, a clear pattern of criminal

associations, double standard loyalties to the war against terrorism
and even treason unfolds a truthful yet another discerning picture
of the neoconservatives war mongering.

Given the nature of circumstances surrounding the Chechens in
Atlanta and the neoconservatives' suspected support for the
Chechens, it is not surprising that there was very little information
focused on the Chechens or Atta's activities in Atlanta.

Yossef Bodansky, a US Congressional intelligence and security
analyst, also testified that the U.S government was vigorously
involved in sponsoring the Chechens for "yet another anti-Russian
jihad" in the "summer of 2000." Numerous neoconservative
members of the American Committee for Peace in Chechnya
(ACPC) in 1999 developed by Richard Perle, Stephen Solarz and
Zbigniew Brzezinski aggressively supported the Chechens during
the summer of 2000. Arms shipments to the Chechens, especially
those in my report from October to December, could easily be
shipped through Turkey and Georgia. Sibel Edmonds testified in
her deposition that members of ATC were involved with
providing arms to groups in Central Asian countries which
included Georgia and other Caspian regions. One of Marc
Grossman's staff members was Major Douglas Dickerson, the
weapons procurement specialist to Central Asia (which includes
Georgia), played a central role in attempts to recruit Edmonds into
ATC. Weapons Procurement Specialist is a fancy name for arms
dealer. The Stinger missiles the Chechens were allegedly in

possession of would be acquired through specialists like Major Dickerson.

These circumstances left clear cut patterns implicating members of ATC and ACPC as accessories to 911. This was their main motive to prevent Al Qaida's Chechen alliance from being implicated as co-conspirators of 911. The timing added a clear motive to undermine investigations into the Chechen connections that the FBI agents in Minnesota and Phoenix were pursuing and last but not least my report to the FBI Atlanta field office Dec. 30, 2000.

On the other hand, Masry was an extremely important contact which there was little mention in the 911 commission. It is highly plausible that Masry served as another contact and support between Khattab, BIF and Zacarias Moussaoui. Masry handled finances to Al Qaida and Chechens through BIF.

Because Masry was alleged by Israeli and U.S Neocon rightwing sources, as an AQ member trained by Iran and Hezbollah and described as a liaison between AQ, Chechens and Iranian supported Hezbollah while Cheney and Israel's hunger for targeting Iran grew there were too many parallels to the fabricated AQ/Saddam Hussein intelligence connections that helped lead 41 countries to war in Iraq. My December 2000 report on the Chechens and the Russian nuclear engineer combined with false or vague allegations of Chechen/Al Qaida liaison Al Masry, Ali Mohammed and other AQ members' training with Hezbollah, phony media reports of Iranians training Chechens and other reports of Chechens in Lebanon in 2006 left an open window for Cheney's crew of intelligence fabricators. These were key elements for twisting and fabricating my report which is why I had no choice but to send warnings to Congress, Senate and Whistleblowers Coalition organizations as proactive prevention of the report from being abused in the same way Saddam Al Qaida connections was abused by people like Douglas Feith, Michael Ledeen, Richard Perle and others.

In the midst of the shady confusions in Atlanta and elsewhere, the report sent to the 'Chief' the first time gave little reaction. Not everyone can claim positions of doing the right thing regardless of their wishful intents. For my boss to receive the report on the first suspect probably put him into a very difficult position. First of all, his responsibilities were milder forms of public safety responses and the safety of his staff and personnel were priorities and not officially counter terrorism. The first part of the report I presented to him was definitely a matter of counter terrorism but since I officially worked under him I felt he needed to know. However, the major and my friend Bobby were a part of a task group or think tank made up of different law enforcement experts and federal agencies, to analyze organized crime and terrorism, affiliated but separate to in regards to the functions of the public safety group. The task group developed and communicated ideas on how visibility and cooperative efforts among agencies and the private sector would deter crime and even the possibilities of any potential terrorist threat which in my case was exactly in line with the task group's intents of visibility, observation, and reporting, and proactive prevention with results of less dramatic circumstances and consequences than the Russians approach to these suspects which was disastrous. That is exactly what happened despite moments of ulcer kicking situations realizing who we were dealing with. The task group was an analytical and advisory group, NOT an active operational force that goes after organized criminals or terrorists. Since the task group was interconnected with and had local and federal agents they could easily circulate the information within the report to Federal law enforcement supervisors in charge that had the jurisdiction to follow up with this particular situation. At least that was the idea I had in mind when I handed the report to him in the first place. The quagmire was that his position was caught between a rock and a hard place and had to balance issues with the shady culture within law enforcement in Atlanta and especially his close relationships to some of the officers that worked off duty in uniform at some of the shady nightclubs. He had been an officer and leader within a law enforcement agency's special operations department for many years. He was and still is a good boss for those who work under him. He was seemingly conservatively strict but in a good sense. His experience and leadership is admirable. He always had a great way of balancing the good from the bad and fine tuning his protégé's which again turned into good leaders. The public safety group is and will be a fantastic contribution to the city especially with leaders like him and the other sergeants and colleagues. However, the chief was a careerist and could not do much without risking anything to do the right thing.

Nonetheless, no matter how impressive people's careers may seem, if they are entrapped in a catch 22 web of corrupt circumstances their decision making will be determined by the corrupt conditions that surrounds them. Therefore, with the corrupt conditions from the Mayor's corruption charges down to law enforcement departments plagued with their own corrupt officers, constructive decisions on how to handle these suspects would be severely compromised.

The situation with the presence of this notoriously violent Interpol suspect was a really extreme situation and not to mention a potential career killer with hair thin risks for any ranking agent or officer to take charge of this case given these Chechens past history of terrorism and mass casualties. This was the most plausible reason why there was little reaction by higher ranking officials to sanction responses to investigate pre 911 suspects. They did not want to risk their careers dealing with this case or these suspects. There were too many interconnecting elements of corruption and mismanagement. After 911, all of the highest ranking officials who had pre-911 knowledge of suspects and warnings were left with formidable choices to tell the truth and accept responsibility which would have ruined, stained their careers and charges brought against them for criminal negligence or cover their negligence up all together. This is the most realistic assessment of any 911 conspiracies.

Neocon Chronicles of Disaster

"Political and religious arrogance extends beyond the boundaries of any fundamental madness." Author

Terrorists attacked America by flying several planes into the twin towers, then the Pentagon, killing several thousands and a failed attempt that killed almost two hundred. Retaliation against the enemy was inevitable. There was an abundance of pissed off people and "gung ho" to go to war. Support for war against Al Qaida and other terrorist groups needed little convincing. Retaliation and vengeance was the only answer. To begin with, there was little "doubt" who the evil culprits were, Osama bin Laden and his cold blooded gang of terrorists. The natural objective was clear; target Al Qaida and Taliban in Afghanistan. Some members of Congress, intelligence agencies, law enforcement and military who inherently distanced themselves from the realization of the destructive road to be, were also the preemptive force whistling and blowing horns before everything went so bad. As always reflective of destructive circumstances, everyone is always smarter after the cause of disastrous events. They knew there were more suspected partners such as the Saudis and Pakistanis involved, but Bush, Cheney and the Neocons had too many invested interests and partnerships with them to accuse them of any foul play.

From the beginning, the Bush administration left little to the imagination that they made it quite clear that the Justice Department could investigate anything the Bush & co approved to pursue. Any concurring investigations, shedding light on issues that would interfere with their plans, agendas or goals with various alliances that would under normal circumstances be investigated by the Justice Department as criminal, were obstructed.

Between the Bush administration and then Attorney General John Ashcroft and FBI Director Robert Mueller, there were clear motives for their obstructions related to the many warnings before 911 and the investigations after. Even immediately after 911, the Justice department did their best to cover for the diplomatic relations with Bush's Saudi friends and business partners, Osama bin Laden family and others, by flying them out soon after 911.[180] Bush jr had substantial financial difficulties in generating success as a businessman in the oil industry. His father's friends, the Saudis, had bailed Bush jr out several times from bankruptcy by investing in Bush jr's company Harken. Those Saudi friends were the Bin Laden family. Two Saudi investors that bailed Bush out were Osama bin Laden's older brother Salem and brother of OBL's wife, Khaled bin Mahfouz. Khaled bin Mahfouz had been placed under investigation for major contributions to OBL's welfare and charity organizations.

---

[180] Leaving so soon? Geraldine Sealey Salon.com (accessed April 20, 2009)

"Khaled bin Mahfouz is a Saudi banker with a 20 percent stake in BCCI, a bank that will go bankrupt a few years later in the biggest corruption scandal in banking history (see BCCI Affair)."[181]

"Wall Street Journal in 1991 states it "raises the question of an effort to cozy up to a presidential son." Two major investors in Bush's company during this time are Salem bin Laden, Osama bin Laden's oldest brother, and Khaled bin Mahfouz." [Salon, 11/19/01 , Intelligence Newsletter, 3/2/00][182]

This is probably one of the main reasons why Osama bin Laden has been able to evade and escape attempts on his life when CIA's Special Activities Division (SAD) teams has had him in their sights and could have taken him out several times but ordered not to by both Clinton and Bush. [183]

Business friends of Bush and Cheney that were flown out soon after 9/11 could have answered critical questions of 9/11. This would be only the beginning of the many dark conspiracies shedding light after that tragic day of September 11th.

---

[181] The BCCI Affair; A Report to the Committee on Foreign Relations United States Senate by Senator John Kerry and Senator Hank Brown December 1992 102d Congress 2d Session Senate Print 102-140

[182] "The United States of oil"; No administration has ever been more in bed with the energy industry -- but does that mean Big Oil is calling Bush's shots? By Damien Cave, Salon.com (accessed April 20, 2009)

[183] CIA videos reveal the missed chances to kill Bin Laden Wrangles stopped arming of plane Yosri Fouda and Nick Fielding The Sunday Times September 4, 2005

Basaev's partner Ibn al Khattab was supported by Saudi and Pakistani organizations through the Al Baraka Bank, Benevolent International foundation and World Assembly of Muslim Youth (WAMY).[184] Any form of Chechen involvement in 911 was disputed despite volumes of information and reports of him being a lieutenant of Al Qaida and a bin Laden confident. Osama bin Laden's family members Abdullah Awad (board member) and Omar Mohammad Awad and Shafiq bin Laden were organizers of the U.S branch of WAMY.[185] All three were on the flight out of the U.S after 911.[186]

"Anonymous sources have said that the Bush administration told FBI investigators to 'back off' when it came to investigating bin Laden's family", forcing an end to the investigation of WAMY, Abdallah and Omar bin Laden that began in 1996 and reopened after 911."

According to Senator Frank Lautenberg (New Jersey) and Senator Charles Schumer's (New York) inquiries into the bin Laden flight after 911, WAMY's address, formerly at 5134 Leesburg Pike, Alexandria VA) in Falls Church, Virginia during the 1990s, was also the same neighborhood where 4 of the 911 hijackers resided

---

[184] USA V. Enaam M. Arnaout, 10/6/2003, pp.24-25/
J. Millard Burr and Robert O. Collins, Alms for Jihad: Charity and Terrorism in the Islamic World (Cambridge: Cambridge University Press, 2006) pp. 45-46.
[185] Spreading Saudi Fundamentalism in U.S. Network of Wahhabi Mosques, Schools, Web Sites Probed by FBI By Susan Schmidt Washington Post Staff Writer Thursday, October 2, 2003; Page A01

just a few blocks down the street. Two bin Laden brothers who were FBI suspects also resided close to WAMY's address.[187] But as immediate reports following 9/11 demonstrated, Bush made sure that many pages involving their Saudi and Pakistani interests were blackened out leaving too many unanswered questions. They simply did not want anyone to know that their partners collaborated with the same terrorists that killed so many Americans on 911. After all they couldn't have Americans believing that they were in bed with the enemy, especially when they needed the main excuse "War against terrorism" to sell their agendas on their fellow countrymen.

Same happened with the 9/11 Commission report. The Commission in the first place was argued by many as biased with the exception of the Bush administration.

Senator Max Cleland was so discontent with the lack of truth and cover ups that he resigned from the Commission in protest.[188] He had really good reason to resign. Max Cleland was Senator of

---

[186] Plane Carried 13 Bin Ladens Manifest of Sept. 19, 2001, Flight From U.S. Is Released *By Dana Milbank* Washington Post Staff Writer Thursday, July 22, 2004; Page A07
[187] Press Release of Senator Lautenberg, Lautenberg, and Schumer: Why Was a Charter Plane Also Rented by White House Used to Fly Bin Laden Family Out of USA After 9/11? Friday, July 23, 2004
[188] "The president ought to be ashamed"; Former Sen. Max Cleland blasts Bush's "Nixonian" stonewalling of the 9/11 commission, his "lies" about Iraq, and his flight-suit photo op on the USS Lincoln after "hiding out" during Vietnam. By Eric Boehlert
http://dir.salon.com/story/news/feature/2003/11/21/cleland/index.html

Georgia until 2003 losing in a battle of smear campaigns by the current Senator Chambliss.

Senator Cleland had every right to know the truth due to the 9/11 suspects in Atlanta and the Chechen report I sent.

Back then, I never really thought of sending my report directly to Senator Cleland's office because I expected that federal law enforcement agencies who were supposed to handle these issues should have sufficed. In most occasions it still is, but like any other organization they have their differences, knots, tangles and even rotten apples. It shouldn't be an excuse, but unfortunately it's the reality of red tape bureaucracy. The rotten apples in high end positions of the Bush Neocon reign were clearly affected by the virus of universal arrogance and ignorance that spread like a disease. The negative critique that stamped the FBI or other agencies as completely incompetent was false and unnecessary. Field agents who put every effort in their jobs and risk their necks investigating suspects of terrorism or organized crime are often caught in on the wire decisions between the harsh realities they face in the underworld and red tape bureaucracy of politics. The few in charge that made decisions by partial loyalty to Bush and Cheney's administration and protecting their careers were arrogant, ignorant and blessed with holy nobility that sustained the quagmires of incompetence. The same quagmire also functions with Democrat administrations.

CIA and SAD teams with Special Forces had done an incredible job of ousting Taliban and Al Qaida with a few including Bin Laden escaping to isolated safe havens in the Pakistani province of Waziristan. It was at this point in time that the U.S and allies failed to take opportunity to help Afghanistan with reconstruction efforts to build their own economic independence and security. As many insisted focusing more attention on al Qaida in Afghanistan and Pakistan, Bush and Cheney evidently insisted on focusing a case for war with Iraq.[189] This was the greatest catastrophic failure of his administration and domino effect leading to financial disaster.

---

[189] Bush and Blair made secret pact for Iraq war; Decision came nine days after 9/11 Ex-ambassador reveals discussion David Rose The Observer, Sunday 4 April 2004 12.20 BST

Chronicles of Forging Intelligence

"Most people in this world do stupid and evil things to others are because they lack the knowledge to know any better. If they knew better good people would not resort to the stupidity and evil of today's deceptions. Therefore, learning and understanding one's own capacity to understand should be spent with attentive thought over one's own actions towards others. Tyrants know none of this due to their excessive grandiosity, but are soulless and shameless in their actions and callous being." Author of book

September 11, 2001, and the few years after wasn't really a rude awakening for many people all over the world and especially in the US, it was the beginning of emblazoned reactions of confined wrath before anyone could come slowly to their rationale and senses.

The neoconservative march of Machiavellian pragmatism paved with reckless and apparent criminally negligent decisions sponsored by Bush and Cheney have distinctively devoured the eight years with ultimate destruction and left a catastrophic inheritance for all to live with.

The Iraq war, even with the courageous and distinguished efforts of most within the armed forces and allies with some tip of the iceberg successes, the disastrous cons by far outweighed the pro's of benefits and failed much due to the civilian decisions of Bush and Cheney's administration and their persistence to support corrupt no bid contractors and private military companies who have reaped fortunes at the expense of everyone else who has endured enormous sacrifice.

The failure wasn't being there in Iraq and taking down Saddam. It was forging lies that conditioned the case for war. It was the many abuses, fraud and mismanagement by many of the contracting companies like Halliburton, KBR and many others fueling and forging conditions and cultures of corruption. Continued widespread corruption of leaders in Baghdad chosen by the Bush administration that sparked internal conflicts and secular feuding between Sunni's and Shia. Al Qaida and other Iraqi resistance groups gained foothold over sections of Baghdad and other areas of Iraq, which fueled recruitment and generated consensus against occupation. While allied special operations forces were in the process of destroying Al Qaida in Afghanistan and Pakistan, roughly 80% of AQ's structure had been wiped out, the Iraq war regenerated new life for Al Qaida led by Zarqawi and allowed them to gain a strong presence in Iraq after the war started thanks to the reckless determination by the Bush administration. Al Qaida would not have gained the strength they did had it not been for all the corruption and mass confusion they were able to exploit. The new revival and trend had turned Al Qaida into franchises of independent cells of self radicalized terrorists and volunteers from all over the world.

U.S and allied operational forces would have succeeded in dramatically reducing volatile conditions catalyzing terrorism, but politically Bush and Cheney needed the fear of terrorism to validate their illegal torture, surveillance programs and other dirty agendas. Terrorism became more of a political ally than a foe. Terrorism was for them a great marketing scheme.

'Terrorists are gonna come get you, kill you and your families. They are going to use weapons of mass destruction against you. Terrorists are going to destroy your way of life.' These notions may be true, but the difference is that those true to fighting or defending against terrorism don't make friends or conduct business with them. The other difference is that terrorists are still a substantial minority compared to criminals, corruption and any other underworld entities apart from pure hardcore terrorists. In fact most of the terrorists the west is at war against are a source of its own monster created by the underworld corruption, greed and false occupation.

The Neocon suspects, displayed in Sibel Edmonds State Secrets Privilege gallery were suspected of criminal activities such as trading national security secrets and accessories by receiving funds from international drug trafficking for lobbying activities through their networks in Israel, Turkey, Pakistan, central Asia and the Caucasus.[190]

---

[190] Sibel Edmonds' State Secrets Privilege Gallery on website JUST A CITIZEN http://justacitizen.com/

Members of the Neocon cliques and their Non Government Organizations (NGO's) have been specifically in the spotlight of official investigations over the years with continuous allegations of treason and conducting business and providing support to networks of terrorists we are at war against. Rogue spawns of every major super power and their intelligence agencies, corporations and sponsorships of war torn cultures gave birth to the new generation of terrorism. These circumstances and entities became the father, mother and family of threats of the latest generations. Many of these business interests with these murky onslaughts were gained through the now outlawed Bank of Commerce and Credit international (BCCI) or also known as Bank of Crooks and Criminals International. Corrupt banking was not born with BCCI nor did it die with it. Within its networks, members, patrons and business associates of the Bush family played a pivotal role in creating evil entities in order to defeat other evil entities. This has become the inheritance and legacy of consequence and disaster Americans and others in the world face today.

Even though the Bush administration could not ignore Osama bin Laden and Al Qaida after 911, using Saddam Hussein as a scapegoat for Al Qaida seemed to be the easy but disparate choice for many reasons including overshadowing Bush's alleged business ties and debts to Bin Laden.

Hawk of Pandora

For years, two major pains of foreign policy were Bin Laden and Saddam Hussein. Because Saddam Hussein began revolting against his original backers against Iran in the 80's, Bush, Cheney and Rumsfeld found him to be an easy marker. Apart from the fear that Saddam possessed WMD's, there were also several other motivations for targeting Iraq. Oil reserves in Iraq were believed to be huge which U.S needed, at least Bush and Cheney's oil cronies, and the other was to insure a medium against Iranian control of Iraq.

Saddam Hussein had been agitating the world with his treatment of the Iraqi's, especially the Kurdish and Shia population to the north and his fumbled attempt at invading Kuwait during the first gulf war. He was considered public enemy number one in the eyes of many. Iraq was a natural suspect and a far too easy sell. Despite the fact that Saddam Hussein was a horrible dictator simply was not enough for the Bush administration to convince alliances to join them in invading Iraq. They needed intelligence that would build the case that Saddam Hussein was the prime "evil doer" on this planet above bin Laden and Al Qaida. As the Bush administration would have it, Saddam Hussein would be the main dictator sponsoring Al Qaida.[191]

---

[191] False claims of Saddam ties to al Qaida- Seymour M. Hersh, "The Stovepipe," *New Yorker*, October 27, 2003, http://www.newyorker.com/archive/2003/10/27/031027fa_fact?printabl e=true

Office of Special Plans was made just for this cause. The OSP was ordered straight from Rumsfeld and Cheney. There would be no outsider interfering in Cheney's 'special plans' to pin Saddam or any other "evil doers" they chose.

The Right Web; "The Office of Special Plans (OSP) was a short-lived outfit in the Pentagon's Policy office that provided the White House with inaccurate, skewed intelligence linking Iraq and al-Qaida that was used to justify the March 2003 U.S. invasion of Iraq."[192]

Many within the intelligence community claimed that the OSP was developed to "cherry pick" all intelligence they could get their hands on, dissect different pieces and put the pieces of intelligence together that would cater to "clear" intelligence suited to Bush and Cheney's needs and wants. Whether these final reports were twisted and distorted meant nothing as long as the end justified the means.

In the aftermath of forged intelligence discoveries and scandals, there were several intelligence bluffs they were mainly intent on using.

The Neocons networks from East Europe, Middle East, Italy, England and especially the U.S. pumped the main stream media with various stories of Saddam's connections to Al Qaida. The

---

[192] *Office of Special Plans* - Right Web Profile IRC-Political Research Associates; www.rightweb.irc-online.org/

OSP's version of intelligence on Saddam Hussein's ties to Al Qaida had two primary angles.

First came the false claim that Muhammed Atta had met a high ranking Iraqi intelligence officer in Prague.[193] The Atta in Prague connection, according to many intelligence officials, appeared to be a desperate cry for evidence linking Saddam to Al Qaida. No such meeting ever took place except for OSP's illusionary intelligence picking. It didn't stop there!

[193] Blair's just a Bush baby; The US President may like to have Tony by his side, but it's crystal-clear that he isn't listening; plus Sir Robin Auld's White Paper could be revived Nick Cohen, The Observer, Sunday 10 March 2002 03.12 GMT

Quagmire of Mullah Krekar

"Al Qaida and terrorists are a threat that will remain enemies to mankind. So are leaders of ignorance and arrogance that forge lies producing more of the same terrorists." Author of book

Second came U.S. efforts to have Najmuddin Faraj Ahmad, better known as Mullah Krekar, released from Norwegian custody and either extradited to the U.S. run Guantanamo Bay facility or have him deported back to Iraq where U.S. led Iraqi authorities could process him under terrorism charges.

Mullah Krekar, a known leader of an insurgent group called Ansar Al Islam, resided in Norway under political asylum until evidence was provided by various international authorities determining his high ranking membership in Ansar Al Islam. His political asylum was then revoked leaving Norwegian authorities with a substantial and bitter sweet but sticky situation with what to do with him. The U.S. state Department had by then filed Ansar Al Islam as a terrorist group affiliated to Al Qaida and froze assets of a charity organization providing funds to the group. Mullah Krekar is certainly a self confessed terrorist who later openly acknowledged the use of terrorism, training of suicide bombers and admits to have been the leader of Ansar al Islam.[194]

---

[194] "Norwegian Jihad" Produced by ABC Australia Distributed by Journeyman Pictures, November 26, 2007

The notion of openly acknowledging training suicide bombers should have been enough to indict Krekar as a terrorist and have him confined to a prison cell or extradited.

This is where the contradictive quagmire presents itself. The U.S., Australia, and England had all legitimate grounds for having Mullah Krekar extradited, indicted, sentenced and punished for his crimes, especially from his own admissions and all other evidence provided.

On the other hand, because of Bush' and Cheney's lies concerning the invasion of the Iraq war, Krekar became the asset of a devil's advocate.

When Colin Powell introduced Bush and Cheney administrations - not the United States- case for war before the United Nations Security Council, they provided numerous faulty intelligence assessments including the allegation of Krekar's ties to Saddam Hussein. In fact Colin Powell even stated, by Bush and Cheney's demands that Krekar and Ansar al Islam were under Baghdad's directive. This was obviously the biggest clue to hold on to Krekar for safe keeping so that neither he could go out and commit terrorism especially against Norway but also to keep Washington from continuing to forge lies about Krekar's ties between Saddam and Al Qaida. As the torture of Khaled Sheik Muhammed induced false testimonies undermining any legitimate legal processes, so would the same happen to Mullah Krekar forcing false confessions Cheney wanted and needed to justify their case for the Iraq war.

Hawk of Pandora

Norwegian authorities believed it would have been better for him to remain in Norway where they could monitor him and keep him from participating in terrorism whether against Norway or any other country without violating their own humanistic laws.

For those who cringe at the thought of this terrorist walking even semi freely on any street without accountability is not only an insult but a severe crime to any victim who has suffered on account of these terrorists. It is a shame for Krekar to be given the freedom he had even with access to the internet to provide supporters with the psychological support to conduct terrorist acts. After all Mullah Krekar has no problem training and sponsoring suicide bombers to kill as many innocent people as possible and openly admitted it. Norway became known as a country that harbors terrorists rather than hold them accountable. That reputation could have been avoided had they indicted him or at least placed him into confinement. Due to shady intelligence that came out from Washington and Colin Powell's presentation of false intelligence to the U.N Security Council on behalf of the Bush administration, any evidence on Krekar as a terrorist leader presented by the Bush administration would have been deemed as unreliable. The case was thrown out due to "safety problems with witnesses." It was after the trial that Krekar had openly expressed his terrorist history of training suicide bombers.

All in all, Norway did the responsible thing even though many despise the fact that he has not been confined and held accountable for his crimes. However, the Bush administration was hardly the ones to lecture Norway about harboring or allowing terrorist suspects or supporters to go free. The Bush and Cheney administration made sure that members of the bin Laden family-their business partner- including Osama bin Laden's brother, who had provided finances to al Qaida and 911, to go free and escorted them out of the country after 911 with the approval of the National Security Council and assistance of Justice Department.[195] They had obstructed connections to the Chechens before and after 911. They had blocked investigations into Pakistani involvement of 911. They had obstructed investigations into ATC members' involvement with sponsors of terrorism. They had committed what most would have considered treason and exposed Valerie Plame as a CIA NOC officer undermining investigations into national security breaches and nuclear terrorism.

Bush and Cheney who were openly ardent about killing terrorists and wanted this terrorist dead, they would have had ample opportunity to do so but Mullah Krekar was clearly more important to them alive than dead.

U.S. was unable to convince Norway after many attempts and a lot of pressure to have him extradited to the U.S. or even deported to Iraq. U.S. was clearly intent on their "interrogation programs" and death sentence and so was Iraq. Norway's laws and policies

---

[195] Saudis flown Out of US 9/13/01 Under FBI Supervision
http://www.saintpetersburgtimes.com/2004/06/09/Tampabay/TIA_now_verifie
s_flig.shtml

of following international treaties are clear in regards to extraditing or deporting any criminal or terrorist to countries that have the death penalty or where torture is practiced.

Unofficially it was clear that, even though Krekar was proven to be a member of a terrorist organization, the Bush administration clearly needed him as another cherry picked excuse to connect Saddam Hussein to Al Qaida. Even that connection would have resulted in a forged or fabricated alliance because Ansar al Islam had no relations with Saddam whatsoever and was even regarded as an enemy. In fact they were at war against Saddam Hussein's Baathist Party. The only vague coinciding claim they incited was that Ansar al Islam involvement in targeting U.S. military personnel also targeted Shia Muslims in North on Iraq/Iran border. They attempted to connect Ansar al Islam's alleged chemical weapons facility, discovered by SAD teams in the Kurdish territories of Iraq, paralleled with claims that Iraqi intelligence provided al Qaida members with biological, chemical and radiological training.[196] All proved to be false.

A small US intelligence extra ordinary rendition team on orders by the Bush administration had attempted to pull a "Snatch and Grab" operation of Krekar in Oslo between April and August,

---

[196] Allegations of Iraqi intelligence providing al Qaida in Biological, Chemical and Radiological training Senate Report on Prewar Intelligence of Iraq, page 329 http://intelligence.senate.gov/phaseiiaccuracy.pdf

2003.[197] The operation was "burned" when Krekar's lawyer received a tip of the impending snatch and grab operation.

The CIA Rendition unit had all the blessings of operating under instructions by Cheney, Rumsfeld and their own intelligence enclaves to apprehend high value targets. Their objective seemed specifically catered to the intelligence needed by Office of Special Plans (OSP) which was tailored by chief intelligence fabricators Douglas Feith, Paul Wolfowitz, Lewis Libby, Larry Franklin, Michael Ledeen and Richard Perle. The original members of OSP were Paul Wolfowitz, Douglas Feith, Abram Shulsky, David Wurmser, Michael Maloof, Steven Cambone and William Luti. Richard Perle served as an adviser to OSP and was at the same time serving as member of the Pentagon's Defense Policy Board.[198] Colin Powell's February 5, 2003 U.N speech using so many false intelligence claims as arguments for invading Iraq specifically directed by Cheney and Rumsfeld but partially tailored by the CIA meant that they needed to find suited intelligence to back their claims regardless of whether they were false intelligence.

---

[197] "Norwegian intelligence knew of CIA agents". Aftenposten *2006-08-01*. http://www.aftenposten.no/nyheter/iriks/article1406229.ece. Retrieved on 2009-04-20. translation, mirror
[198] Sourcewatch, Office of Special Council

Hawk of Pandora

The rendition team was made up of veteran CIA agents from the Iran Contra days.[199] The two agents from this team that were exposed in Oslo were Gregory Asherleigh, 50 yrs., arrived in April, 2003 and Cynthia Logan, 45 yrs. arrived June, 2003.[200] The Rendition team leader Robert Seldon Lady, who was wanted by Interpol in Italy for the illegal abduction of an Egyptian Cleric and other charges, was also implicated in the Niger Yellow Cake forgeries allegedly on behalf of Michael Ledeen that served with Richard Perle and Douglas Feith in the Office of Special Plans. According to an article by The Times (London), a SISMI (Italian Intelligence) asset used to pass on the Niger Yellow cake documents was quoted, "I was told a woman in the Niger embassy (which was a small apartment) in Rome had a gift for me. I met her and she gave me documents. SISMI wanted me to pass on the documents but they didn't want anyone to know they had been involved." [201] There has been substantial controversy alleging that the "woman" (which is 'lady' in Italian) was the CIA station chief in Milan, Robert Seldon Lady. The alleged "Lady" staff member at the Nigerian Embassy has never been investigated or identified making her a nonexistent character and witness within an extremely important case. The forgeries were then passed on to a

---

[199] "Extraordinary rendition" -The hunt for "Mister Bob" and the 18 bastards By: Fausto Giudice 11/18/05 Translated from French by Ragnar B. Johannessen
[200] Suspect CIA agents were in Norway by Jonathan Tisdall Aftenposten http://www.aftenposten.no/english/local/article1397884.ece?service=print
[201] Italian spies 'faked documents' on Saddam nuclear purchase By Nicholas Rufford The Sunday Times August 1, 2004

female investigative reporter for Panorama who then passed it onto the U.S. Embassy in Rome. Michael Ledeen was a contributing writer for Panorama.

Michael Ledeen had also served with Richard Perle on the American Committee for Peace in Chechnya.[202] Michael Ledeen also had an interest in the Chechen report. Michael Ledeen was also one of the main players in the Iran Contra scandal. In 1984, Michael Ledeen proposed the idea of setting the illegal arms sales to Iran using Manucher Ghorbanifar, the arms trafficker, to make it happen. Oliver North testified that it was Ledeen that proposed to send the funds to the Contras from that Arms deal with Iran.[203] Robert S Lady is a native of Honduras born in Tegucigalpa and raised there till he moved on to New Orleans and became a law enforcement officer for New Orleans PD.[204] Robert Lady was allegedly the CIA contact that made sure the funds were delivered to the Contras. Lady was allegedly in charge of the notorious death squad "Battalion 316" that was responsible for abductions and torture of anti American dissidents and communists in Nicaragua. [205] This is clearly why he was given responsibility for the extraordinary rendition unit regarding his past history.

---

[202] American Committee for Peace in Chechnya: Members
http://www.peaceinchechnya.org/about_members.htm
[203] Walsh, LE (1993-08-04), *Final Report of the Independent Counsel for Iran/Contra Matters; volume I: "Investigations and Prosecution"*, Washington, D.C.
[204] Bob, 007 senza limiti. Chi lo ha coperto? Guido Olimpio 24 giugno 2005 *Corriere della Sera*
[205] Ibid

Hawk of Pandora

Robert Lady was clearly in alliance with Ledeen and liaison as the CIA's station chief in Milan. Lady was certainly a plausible player involved with the Niger Yellow cake forgeries to begin with. Michael Ledeen with his close ties to Italian Intelligence and Government was primarily the suspect OSP member that played a major role in the Niger Yellow Cake forgery through his Italian intelligence connections in Italy. The Niger forgeries originated from the Niger embassy in Rome. Lady also had a close working relationship with Mario Scaramella and his partner.[206]

The Italian newspapers La Republica with reporters Carlo Bonini and Giuseppe D'Avanzo, who first busted the Niger Yellow cake story, had run stories of phone interceptions between Mario Scaramella and Italian police, the CIA station chief in Milan and another CIA agent in Rome.[207]

From the interceptions from the phone calls according to newspaper Corriere della Sera, it became comprehensible that Lady had been in contact with Mario Scaramella. Mario Scaramella, a consultant to the Mitrokhin commission in Italy, was deeply and directly involved with the Litvinenko case and was a close associate to Alexander Litvinenko and Boris Berezovsky.[208]

---

[206] "How one man insinuated himself into poisoning case" *International Herald Tribune* 9 January 2007.
[207] Il falso dossier di Scaramella - "Così la Russia manipola Prodi", *La Repubblica*, 11 January 2007
[208] ibid

These connections sustained a clear line of interests on all players in the field related to the Niger Yellow cake to Sibel Edmonds case of the ATC members Richard Perle to Michael Ledeen to Robert Seldon Lady and then to the Rendition unit that were present in Oslo led by Lady. Krekar was one, and I certainly had to suspect that my report (not me) was the other given the major significance of the Chechen report which was evident by the subject based data mining attack on my computer June 23 via my adsl service provider that used Global Crossings fiber optic technology at the same time that the CIA rendition team were present in Norway.

Global Crossings intelligence technology was based on IP data mining which was consistent with the attack on my computer. The CIA agents from the Rendition team had access to the extensive and wide scope capabilities of Net-Centric Warfare networks – in the same way as Able Danger was - using subject-based data mining as a tool to gather relationship information from their targets.

"Subject-based data mining" is a data mining technique involving the search for associations between individuals in data. In context of combating terrorism, the National Research Council provides the following information: "Subject-based data mining uses an initiating individual or other datum that is considered, based on other information, to be of high interest, and the goal is to determine what other persons or financial transactions or movements, etc., are related to that initiating datum."[209]

As a result of being the author of a highly important report concerning the Chechen suspects (i.e. the possibility of nuclear terrorism by them) related to 911, I instantly became a person of high interest. More so, it was evident they needed to find out who covered my back and who else knew - specially the intelligence officer that (uninvolved with the case became an instant witness to the suspects) was with me at the nightclub who noticed the other Interpol and unidentified suspects (Surikov and Saidov) on the other side of the bar - about the Chechens at the nightclub and other witnesses elsewhere. Like I said I had broke off all contacts with these witnesses just for reasons like this. I had already left too many temporary loose ends for any such plausible contingency to take place and despite their mighty data mining or surveillance programs they would still have problems finding who all the loose ends were. As a natural born Brooklyn ball busting stubborn blooded Viking from New York I felt it was my responsibility to protect the constitution against foreign and domestic enemies. As far as I was concerned the neoconservatives whether republican or democrat had clearly demonstrated a history of treasonous activities and consistent business associations with people known to have supported terrorism. That

---

[209] National Research Council, Protecting Individual Privacy in the Struggle Against Terrorists: A Framework for Program Assessment, Washington DC: National Academies Press, 2008.

constitutes domestic enemy. The way they have treated and destroyed the careers and lives of whistleblowers to cover for their own criminal negligence, protecting the identities of these witnesses at any cost to myself became a sacred responsibility. This also helped sustain reasonable protection and integrity of my report from potential abuse from people like Ledeen and Perle. I was concerned about influence peddling in my social network to gain any other information about others associated to these reports.

Ledeen's partner Perle had both ownership and extensive influence over several companies that specialized in data mining (surveillance) technology, including Global Crossing. The CIA rendition agents in Oslo were obviously under specific instructions from Bush and Cheney's internal intelligence apparatus influenced by members and advisers of OSP and DPB which included Feith, Ledeen and Perle on behalf of Cheney through the CIA. The rendition operations were in fact sanctioned under 'Executive Orders' which is a presidential order. Krekar was certainly high value for OSP's efforts to forge or fabricate evidence linking Saddam to Al Qaida. My report was either a sore loose end that they needed to hush down or would have been easy intelligence to sell if they could twist the circumstances around my report much like they did with many other reports. Because alleged reports by Israeli and U.S Neocon rightwing sources began surfacing that Masry was allegedly trained in Iran by

Hezbollah and as a liaison between AQ, Chechens and Iranian supported Hezbollah, there were too many parallels to the fabricated AQ/Saddam Hussein intelligence connections that helped lead 41 countries to war in Iraq. My December 2000 report on the Chechens and the Russian nuclear engineer combined with false or vague allegations of Chechen/Al Qaida liaison Al Masry, Ali Mohammed and other AQ members' training with Hezbollah, media reports of Iranian Republican Guard training Chechens and other reports of Chechens left an open window for Cheney's crew of intelligence fabricators to take advantage of. These were key elements for twisting and fabricating my report which is why I had no choice but to send warnings to Congress, Senate and powerful whistleblower coalition organizations that have some clout with highest levels of Congress.

My report was in fact very attractive, very vulnerable and very sustainable for abuse. They had already tried to play the Al Qaida/Saddam connection several times, especially with Krekar. Cheney even added the Saddam/Al Qaida connection with nuclear terrorism in his speeches several times. Cheney and his neocons were also extremely trigger happy with targeting Iran and needed catered intelligence, so there was no reason why they wouldn't try to pull it off with my Chechen report.

For obvious reasons I had to suspect Michael Ledeen, Richard Perle and Marc Grossman pulling the strings of their connections in Norway was that Michael Ledeen, Richard Perle and Marc Grossman had a stake involving the Chechens and they had close business associations to Global Crossings. Ledeen had close influential associations to most of these elements and leader of the rendition unit.

Richard Perle had to resign as chair member from the Defense Policy Board (DPB) and Global Crossings as a result of conflicting business interests with Global Crossings and "ethics violations." Perle remained as a member of DPB which meant that they presented advice on major strategic military policies - including surveillance of terrorists or people they regarded as a risk to their policies residing overseas including allied countries. It was here that Richard Perle –in collaboration with OSP members and Douglas Feith, who was deputy SecDef - was among fundamental influences in the decision to go to war in Iraq. Marc Grossman was tightly connected to the Cohen Group which also had close interests with Global Crossings. William Cohen was Director of Global Crossings Asia and board member of Global Crossings international. Marc Grossman is now serving as Vice Chairman of the Cohen Group.[210] Marc Grossman was in Oslo in 2002 while Richard Perle visited a small town called Gol in Hallingdal, Norway, in 2004 only few hours away from my town of residence I moved to after 911.[211] [212] Some of the locals -

---

[210] Marc Grossman, Vice Chairman of Cohen Group
http://www.cohengroup.net/about/teammember.cfm?id=5
[211] Grossman, Traavik Meet in Oslo on NATO Enlargement, Summit, April 19, 2002; Norwegian Ministry of Foreign Affairs Oslo, Norway April 19, 2002
http://italy.usembassy.gov/viewer/article.asp?article=/file2002_04/alia/A20423
04.htm

members of a group (unsuspected at the time) I had become acquainted with – were later suspected of being in direct contact with or collaborating with assets of the suspected neoconservatives - had convinced me to use and helped to sign me up with the adsl service provider within two weeks prior to the data mining incident. Two relatives from the same group spent the same weekend Perle was in the town of Gol, Norway. I also traced very few strings of Facebook friends of these locals directly to Daniel Pipes, another neoconservative member of American Committee for Peace in Chechnya and close associate to Richard Perle and Michael Ledeen.

Bush, Cheney and Rumsfeld were fiercely insistent upon convincing the world that Saddam Hussein had weapons of mass destruction and ties to Al Qaida.

Cheney was apparently so furious at times because he couldn't get the twisted intelligence he needed, that he was known for intentionally targeting everyone that refused to cooperate. He expended substantial resources in the U.S. and overseas to insure that those who got in the way were retaliated for their opposition to his goals.

Cheney's goals? Cheney's obsessively outspoken rhetoric about terrorism covered by the administrations cheerleaders of

---

[212] Møte med fyrsten Richard Perle snakker med lav, behagelig stemme. Men det han sier, er egnet til å skremme. By HALVOR ELVIK Published Friday 27 February, 2004 Dagbladet News

warmongers and profiteers seemed like he would have embraced the idea of more terrorist acts such as a suicide bombing campaign in Europe to convince the wealthy European countries (like Norway) to add more resources with the "war on terrorism". Cheney had clear political and financial motives to give an appearance of fighting terrorism while earning large revenues from supporting it behind the curtain. Those who risked everything to expose and stop the deep, dark and corrupt policies of Cheney and his henchmen and their behind the curtain support for terrorism were his enemies.

The Bush administration was only part of the problem as there have been many other variables inciting catastrophic consequences in the U.S and around the world.

The combination of counter cultures, corrupt, criminal and terrorist elements from any side to the average individual that gets caught in between the web of these destructive elements play important roles that undermine stability anywhere and is the essence of what triggers conflicts that occur in this world. It isn't a conspiracy of a grand 'new world order' network but various elements of underworld, corporate, political and religious needs for supply and demand that conditions social destructive circumstances. Are specific ideals, religions or politics at fault? Is the right or left wing at fault? Are the arms or oil industry at fault? Are the war mongers at fault? Are the corporations at fault? Are authorities or governments at fault? Are countercultures from either side at fault? Are terrorists at fault? It is all of the above! It's the paradox of Pandora's Box and humans are Pandora! Pandora is the key keeper to the box of hope or the demons locked within it. Humans are the release of hope or the contents of our destruction.

Upcoming book

Hawk of Pandora: A 911 Missing Link Volume II

Preview

A lot of things were happening back in the states. We were
already at war with Iraq, and a psychological war between Bush,
Cheney, the neoconservatives and their crony intelligence clique
and corporate patrons brewed against the rational intelligence
community alongside national security whistleblowers.

The Valerie Plame case, Sibel Edmonds case, members of Able
Danger, U.N weapons inspectors, some members of National
Security Council and whistleblowers from federal and intelligence
agencies and members of Congress expressed serious allegations
of crimes against the Bush administration. Righteously so! The
Bush administration had been up to their necks in alleged criminal
conspiracies that they seemed to go back and forth from offensive
back to defensive while their Neocon intelligence apparatus was
searching for information and intelligence- phony or not- to
confirm Bush and Cheney's false up front statements. It was
almost as if to spin up intelligence just so they wouldn't be
embarrassed about being wrong.

Back in Trollville I was trying to make heads and tails of the dark
situation back in the U.S. and who was causing so many intrigues
in Trollville.

Events involving members of a local clique and a "group"
eventually left a clear pattern of issues of suspected concerns;

Hawk of Pandora

- 2002; A local businessman and associate of the clique aided a suspected Colombian cocaine trafficker and suspected FARC member with housing and assistance. He was first identified due to an out of the blue irrational threatening outburst towards me yelling Latin profanities about me being a cop from the U.S. After running a check, there was a warrant by the Southern District of New York of a Colombian trafficker from FARC's districts that was an exact match to this Colombian. This suspect was later deported due to his involvement with a small (1kg) shipment of cocaine which was intercepted by a local police raid. Members of the clique had clearly tipped off this Colombian about my background working with law enforcement which gave him a wrong impression that I was a cop or federal agent.

- Members and friends of a local group associated to the clique were involved by aiding or contact with;

✓ June 2003; Member of this group recommended and arranged to set up an adsl service provider that used Global Crossing fiber optic technology. This was before there was any reason to suspect members of this group. The day the ADSL service provider was activated my computer was effected by subject based data mining on June 23. Members of the CIA rendition team were identified in Oslo, Norway from April to August 2003. The leader of the Rendition team was a former Iran Contra veteran and associated to the Neocon clique Michael

Ledeen and Richard Perle (both members of American Committee for Peace in Chechnya [ACPC]).

✓ Close members of this same group were in Gol, Norway the same weekend Richard Perle stayed there the following year Feb. 2004.

✓ A close friend of the same group was contacted by a Baltic woman by late 2004. After establishing a relationship, the woman arranged a trip to meet this friend of the group in a town in the Caucasus where Anton Surikov was present at the time for a Sufi leader conference. This same woman later contacted me in early 2007 and was later identified as an associate of Surikov's partner with his network in Far West.

✓ Autumn 2004; another close friend of this group attended a school co-managed by the pro Israeli Christian Pentecostal movement 'Living Word' that also co-owned and managed the 'Magazinet' which republished the Muhammed cartoons. Living Word is closely associated to John Ashcroft's relatives in Norway. Ulf Ekman, the other co-owner of Magazinet with Living Word is closely associated to members of Christian Pro Israeli rightwing movement in the U.S and Israel that has openly advocated war against Islam.

✓ A member of this same group had close intimate relationships to;

   ▪ A businessman from the Mid East described by the group as a close associate of former Vice President Agnew Spiro and pilot for Pan Aviation which indicated he was an associate or aid with Sarkis Soghanalian, an arms dealer involved with BCCI and Iran Contra scandal and owner of Pan Aviation.

- A former bar owner in Oslo, Norway, tied to the former gang of Arfan Bhatti. His bar according to his statements was frequented by the gang Bhatti was still a member of at the time. Arfan Bhatti was indicted for attacking a Jewish synagogue and planning to attack the U.S and Israeli Embassy.

- Intimate relationships with two North African brothers. The "Group" member and her Living Word connected friend deliberately made me aware of the son of one of these brothers due to his martyr like literature. He was deemed as an attractive target for recruitment as a suicide bomber candidate. This candidate was later recruited to one of the few universities in England Anton Surikov and his partner Ruslan Saidov was associated to through their institute IPROG. Saidov had a history as Chechen intelligence officer, trainer and recruiter of suicide bomber candidates. Friends of the group were suspected of indirectly assisting with his recruitment to this school due to their connections in England. See Engender Burned

- Members of the same group and or clique are suspected of aiding a female agent that contacted me in 2007 prior to Al Gore receiving the Nobel Peace prize. This agent was identified as belonging to the same network that was alleged to have targeted Al Gore and Clintons Builders for Peace organization in the mid 90's and Al Gore's 2000 presidential campaign. Anton Surikov and a CIA associate were alleged to have targeted Al Gore with a disinformation campaign between 1999 and 2000. The father of the suicide bomber candidate I describe in chapter Engender Burned had direct access to the Nobel Peace Prize.

References

1. US v Zacarious Moussaoui Defense Exhibit 129
2. Shamil Basaev Interpol Warrant 1999/14843
3. As Russia was expanding into the Northern Caucasus in the 1800's, it ran into a significant stumbling block: the Islamic warrior - priest, Imam Shamil (1797 - 1871).

"Power Struggle in Checheno - Ingushetia," Ann Sheehy
Report on the USSR
RFE/RL Research Institute, 15 Nov 1991, p. 20.

4. Jihad of Imam Shamil By Kerim Fenari; photograph ?
5. Photo: Natalia Medvedeva, http://exhibition.ipvnews.org/photo_080.php Date: 1995 (Photo: public domain)
6. Interpol file Shamil Basaev 1999/14843/original picture taken from Qoqaz.net
7. Russian discrimination toward peoples from the Caucasus has been well documented. See: "Shamil Basayev - the Lone Wolf," *Moscow News* , No. 24 - 24, 30 Jun - 6 July 1995, p. 4.
8. Women and Transnational Organized Crime Prepared by: Yvon Dandurand and Vivienne Chin *International Centre for Criminal Law Reform and Criminal Justice Policy.* January 2000.
9. *Muslim Resistance to the Tsar: Shamil and the Conquest of Dagestan* Moshe Gammer, (Portland: Frank Cass, 1994).
10. International Trafficking in Women from Central Europe and the NIS, Amy O'Neill, Office of Analysis of Terrorism, Narcotics and Crime, Bureau of Intelligence and Research, US Dept of State, Washington, D.C., December 16, 1997
11. Picture from Qoqaz.net referring to statement from suspect "you die, for 40 day your wife wear!"
12. "Historical Perspective on the Conflict in Chechnia," *Low Intensity Conflict and Law Enforcement* , Robert F. Baumann, Vol 4, No. 1 (Summer 1995).
13. Qoqaz.net Quotes of Wahhab interpretations of Quran, Interview with Chechen Mujahideen 1999
14. Wahhabism http://en.wikipedia.org/wiki/Wahhabism
15. Shamil Basaev and Deputy Ibn al Khattab invaded Dagestan late summer 1999, Nabi (2003)
16. The Jihad of Imam Shamyl By Kerim Fenari p 2
17. *Muslim Resistance to the Tsar: Shamil and the Conquest of Dagestan,* Moshe Gammer, (Portland: Frank Cass, 1994).

18. Reuven Paz, ICT Academic Director Institute of Counter Terrorism
19. Photo: Interpol file 1999/14843
20. Photo: Are Maskhadov and Basaev Planning To Go To Abkhazia, allnews.ru, http://lenta.ru/english/2000/05/17/basaev/
21. Interpol warrant Shamil Basaev file 1999/14843 (warrant has since been altered)
22. Interpol file 14773 of Movsaev Tourpal/Picture Aslan Edisoultanov (Sketch made by myself at the time of identifying suspects)
23. STATEMENT FOR THE RECORD, FBI DIRECTOR ROBERT S. MUELLER III, JOINT INTELLIGENCE COMMITTEE INQUIRY INTRODUCTORY REMARKS before United States Senate Select Committee on Intelligence Sept. 26, 2002.
24. United States of America V Zacarias Moussaoui; THE UNITED STATES DISTRICT COURT FOR THE EASTERN DISTRICT OF VIRGINIA ALEXANDRIA DIVISION, DECEMBER 2001 TERM - AT ALEXANDRIA INDICTMENT
25. "There are no witnesses who report that Moussaoui and Binalshibh actually met in London, but Moussaoui's subsequent travel to Afghanistan implies that he received instructions from Binalshibh. They both resided at the same dorm in London. See ibid. Summary of Penttbom, p. 86., The 911 Commission Report
26. Ibid
27. Ibid
28. The Chechens' American friends John Laughland guardian.co.uk, Wednesday 8 September 2004 23.59 BST
29. Lawless regions in Georgia, Murphy (2004).
30. Trouble in the North Caucasus, Kulikov, General Anatoliy, Fort Leavenworth, Kan.: Foreign Military Studies Office. Originally published in *Military Review,* July–August 1999.
31. CRS Report for Congress; Received through the CRS Web Order Code RS20411
December 7, 1999 Afghanistan: Connections to Islamic Movements in Central and South Asia and Southern Russia Kenneth Katzman Specialist in Middle Eastern Affairs, Foreign Affairs, Defense, and Trade.
32. "Storm in Moscow": A Plan of the Yeltsin "Family" to Destabilize Russia John B. Dunlop The Hoover Institution October 8, 2004 p42
33. "Blowing up Russia" Aleksander Litvinenko and Feltshinski 2006 p

34. Pro-Chechen rebels have carried out hijackings and hostage takings in Turkey, including an April 2001 siege at an Istanbul hotel in which 120 people were held captive for 12 hours before rebels surrendered and released the hostages unharmed. See "Chechens in Theater Raid Linked to Turkish Foundations" (2002).
35. Chechen Parliamentary speaker: Basaev was GRU officer The Jamestown Foundation, September 8, 2006
36. Email between Anton Surikov and Oleg Grechenevsky 09/17/05 http://www.mail-archive.com/cia-drugs@yahoogroups.com/msg01967.html original source from Cf. *Argumenty i Facty*, 9/15/99, http://www.aif.ru/oldsite/986/art010.html.
37. Ibid
38. http://www.pravda.info/news/2695.html
Анатолий Баранов и Антон Суриков вошли в состав руководства агентства « FarWestLtd » - 2005.05.03.
39. *Obituary: Badri Patarkatsishvili*, Tom Parfitt, *The Guardian*, London, 02-15-2008
40. Lithuanian intelligence agencies helped KGB's Mitrokhin to escape to Great Britain- *Lietuvos zinios Vilnius-* Eurasian Secret Services Daily Review 07.10.2007.
41. Annual report 1999, Lithuania International Helsinki Federation of Human Rights.
42. SOVIET TURMOIL; Lithuania's New Defense Minister: Young Man With a Nonviolent Strategy By STEPHEN KINZER, Published: Wednesday, September 4, 1991
43. Yasenev's Memo http://left.ru/burtsev/ops/yasenev_en.phtml
44. "Personnel Announcement". The White House. http://georgewbush-whitehouse.archives.gov/news/releases/2005/02/20050202-10.html.
45. Sutherland, John. "No more Mr Scrupulous Guy". The Guardian. http://www.guardian.co.uk/Archive/Article/0,4273,4358017,00.html.
46. Anton Surikov, *Crime in Russia*, p38-39
47. Albert Einstein Institute
48. "Caucasian diamond traffic" (Moscow, 2005), http://www.civilresearch.org/pdf/7.pdf: "In spring 1997 Adnan Khashoggi introduced Hozh-Ahmed Nukhaev to James Baker."
49. PBS, Frontline; The Dark Side
50. Burtzev.ru

51. "Abkhaz smugglers deliver the drugs by truck to Port Sukhumi on the Black Sea. From there, the drugs are carried by Turkish ships to the port of Famagusta in Northern Cyprus where local drug dealers take over. On the return routes, the ships, truck and helicopters carry arms and munitions acquired by Turkish intelligence for Basaev's forces." CHECHNYA The *Mujahedin* Factor by Yossef Bodansky

52. The above collaborates with Yossef Bodansky's descriptions. Yasenev gives descriptive profile details based on information from IPROG and Forum.msk.ru which Surikov and Saidov are members of http://left.ru/burtsev/ops/yasenev_en.phtml

53. Ibid

54. Ibid

55. Pictures of Adnan Khashoggi and Khoz Ahmed Noukhaev together at a meeting

Caucasian diamond traffic Part 2
http://www.civilresearch.org/pdf/7.pdf: Moscow June 2005.

56. "LUNCH WITH THE CHAIRMAN; Why was Richard Perle meeting with Adnan Khashoggi?" by Seymour M. Hersh Issue of 2003-03-17.

57. Russian Says Kremlin Faked 'Terror Attacks' February 1, 2002, New York Times

58. http://www.baltictimes.com/news/articles/13659/ Berezovsky, Neil Bush, Latvian businessmen meet Sep 23, 2005

59. www.halliburton.com/ps/default.aspx?navid=1225&pageid=2517 -

60. "Cheney Led Halliburton To Feast at Federal Trough" Center for Public Integrity (CPI) at www.public-i.org.

61. "Separatism, Islam and Oil," . Cf. "The tendencies of interregional and international integration in North Caucasia," Caucasian Knot, eng.kavkaz.memo.ru/reginfotext/engreginfo/id/560578.html.

62. "ASSAULT AT HIGH NOON" By John Kohan/Moscow; Dean Fischer/Washington and Yuri Zarakhovich/Moscow Monday, Jun. 26, 1995 Time

63. Basayev has given numerous interviews describing the Budennovs k raid from his perspective. For example, see Foreign Broadcast Information Service: FBIS - SOV - 95 - 116, FBIS - SOV - 95 - 139 and FBIS - SOV - 95 - 142.

64. Ibid

65. Otto Latsis, "Zestokost porozhdaet tol'ko zestokost" Brutality breeds nothing but brutality, Izvestiya, 20 June 95, pp1-2

66. " See: Stepan Kiselev, "Hostages of the Kremlin. The Tragic Event s in Budennovsk are Changing the Political Landscape of Russia," *Moskovskiye novosti*, 18 - 25 June 95, p. 5, as translated in FBIS - SOV - 95 - 141 - S, 24 July 1995.

67. Richard Sakwa, ed (2005). "Western views of the Chechen Conflict". *Chechnya: From Past to Future*. Anthem Press. pp. 235. ISBN 978 1 84331 165 2.

68. "Nuclear materials missing at radon factory" London Sunday Times 1995/ RFE/RL Newsline.

69. Stanislav Lunev. *Through the Eyes of the Enemy: The Autobiography of Stanislav Lunev*, Regnery Publishing, Inc., 1998. ISBN 0-89526-390-4

70. Modernization Of Strategic Nuclear Weapons In Russia: The Emerging New Posture by Nikolai Sokov Monterey Institute for International Studies May 1998

71. The Threat of Nuclear Diversion Statement for the Record by John Deutch, Director of Central Intelligence to the Permanent Subcommittee on Investigations of the Senate Committee on Government Affairs 20 March 1996.

72. Peter Baker, "15 Tied to Al Qaeda Turned over to the U.S.," *Washington Post,* October 22, 2002, p. A17

73. Ibid

74. "Russia calls on Georgia to handover Chechen field commanders," Eurasia.org/Georgia Daily Digest

75. Is Shamil Basaev in Georgia? RFE/RL Newsline Jan. 5 2001

76. Prosecutors Say Corruption in Atlanta Police Dept Is Widespread By SHAILA DEWAN and BRENDA GOODMAN Published: April 27, 2007

77. Ibid

78. Atlanta police officers indicted Kaplan Gambino case Atlanta Journal Constitution June 6, 2001

79. FORMER ATLANTA POLICE OFFICER DAVID FREEMAN SENTENCED TO PRISON IN "DIABLOS" STREET GANG CASE August 08, 2005 www.usdoj.gov/usao/gang/diablos.htm

80. National News Briefs; Sheriff-Elect in Georgia Fatally Shot in Ambush New York Times December 17, 2000

81. The Growing Threat of International Organized Crime...Hearing Before The Subcommittee On Crime Of The Committee On The Judiciary House Of Representatives One Hundred Fourth Congress Second Session January 25, 1996 U.S. GOVERNMENT PRINTING OFFICE WASHINGTON:1996

82. The Body Sellers: Hundreds of Thousands of Illegal Immigrants in Overseas Pipeline, Says State Department." Committee for a Safe Society. (2000, July).
83. High Intensity Drug Trafficking Area (HIDTA) program http://en.wikipedia.org/wiki/HIDTA
84. MEXICO'S DRUG CARTEL MOVES TO U.S.: Atlanta a hub for East Coast Violence is following, but to a lesser extent By Jeremy Schwartz Cox International Correspondent Published on: 08/01/08
85. The Sword and the Shield: The Mitrokhin Archive and the Secret History of the *KGB* by Christopher M. Andrew and Vasili Mitrokhin (Paperback - 8 Aug 2000)
86. Professor Bruce M. Bagley, *Globalization and Transnational Organized Crime: The Russian Mafia in Latin America and the Caribbean*
87. "Chechen terrorists probed" Washington Post, October 13,2004
88. "Cheney, Invoking the Specter of a Nuclear Attack, Questions Kerry's Strength" by Randal C. Archibold, NY Times, October 20, 2004
89. Allison, Graham. Nuclear Terrorism: The Ultimate Preventable Catastrophe. New York: Times Books, 2004
90. "2 Nuclear Experts Briefed Bin Laden, Pakistanis Say" Washington Post, December 12, 2001
91. At The Center Of The Storm (New York: Harper Collins, 2007)
92. Allison, Graham. Nuclear Terrorism: The Ultimate Preventable Catastrophe. New York: Times Books, 2004
93. Symposium: Al Qaeda's Nukes by Jamie Glazov, FrontPage Magazine, October 27, 2006
94. Stanislav Lunev. *Through the Eyes of the Enemy: The Autobiography of Stanislav Lunev*, Regnery Publishing, Inc., 1998. ISBN 0-89526-390-4
95. Ibid
96. "Is Lebed Russia's Loosest Cannon? An Exclusive NBC interview with Alexander Lebed," October 2, 1997, http://www.msnbc.com
97. 'Russian engineer's move to U.S. is like a miracle' by Maria Mallory Atlanta Journal-Constitution, June 21, 2000.
98. Emerging criminal state; Economic and Political Aspects of Organized Crime in Russia by Yuriy A. Voronin pg 56 - Russian Organized Crime; The new threat Edited by Phil Williams
99. New York State Organized Crime Task Force, et al., "An Analysis of Russian Émigré Crime," *Transnational Organized*

Crime 2(2-3) (Summer-Autumn 1996). Russian Organized Crime in The United States By James O. Finckenauer, Ph.D. International Center National Institute of Justice

100. GRU (intelligence) http://warfare.ru

101. Loretta Napoleoni, *Terror Incorporated: Tracing the Dollars Behind the Terror Networks* (New York: Seven Stories Press, 2005), 90-97

102. Ralf Mutschke, "The Threat Posed by the Convergence of Organized Crime, Drugs Trafficking and Terrorism", statement before a hearing of the US House of Representatives Committee on the Judiciary Subcommittee on Crime, December 13, 2000. Mr. Mutschke is the Assistant Director, Criminal Intelligence Directorate, International Criminal Police Organization - Interpol General Secretariat. Web site: http://www.house.gov/judiciary/muts1213.htm.

103. THE PROGRESSIVE, August 1999, Title: "Mercenaries in Kosovo: The U.S. Connection to the KLA" Author: Wayne Madsen; COVERTACTION QUARTERLY, Spring-Summer 1999, Title: "Kosovo `Freedom Fighters' Financed by Organized Crime," Author: Michel Chossudovsky.

104. Sex-slave whistle-blowers vindicated By Robert Capps

105. Nietzsche, Friedrich, *Human, All Too Human*. Cf. Section Two

106. Robert I. Friedman, *Red Mafiya: How the Russian Mob Has Invaded America* (Boston: Little Brown, 2000)

107. The BCCI Affair; A Report to the Committee on Foreign Relations United States Senate by Senator John Kerry and Senator Hank Brown December 1992 102d Congress 2d Session Senate Print 102-140 http://www.fas.org/irp/congress/1992_rpt/bcci/

108. The Israeli "art student" mystery; For almost two years, hundreds of young Israelis falsely claiming to be art students haunted federal offices -- in particular, the DEA. No one knows why -- and no one seems to want to find out. By Christopher Ketcham, Salon.com http://www.salon.com/news/feature/2002/05/07/students/print.html

109. Russian Says Kremlin Faked 'Terror Attacks' By PATRICK E. TYLER
Published: February 1, 2002 NY Times

110. The spies who came in from the art sale *Creative Loafing* has obtained a report detailing alleged Israeli spy activity in the United States. Published 03.20.02 By John Sugg Creative Loafing, Atlanta.

111. Ibid

112. *Red Mafiya: How the Russian Mob Has Invaded America* (Boston: Little Brown & Co., 2000

113. Le Monde, Paris

114. Football Hooligans, and War", Ivan Čolović, Central European University Press, 2000.

115. Official site for Obilić fans, http://home.drenik.net/vitezovi/

116. A Shady Militia Chief Arouses Serbs By CHUCK SUDETIC, New York Times Published: Sunday, December 20, 1992

117. "Gangster's life of Serb warlord" By Balkans correspondent Paul Wood BBC News Saturday, 15 January, 2000

118. Profile: Marko Milosevic, BBC News Monday, 9 October, 2000.

119. Serbs 'used chemical weapons' As British team unearths growing number of atrocities, UN adviser alleges 4,000 Albanians poisoned. by Richard Norton-Taylor and Lucy Ward, The Guardian, Tuesday 24 August 1999 01.45 BST

120. Ibid

121. Serbs threaten to unleash deadly 'secret weapon' ROBERT BLOCK in Belgrade, The Independent *Tuesday, 15 February 1994*

122. Ibid

123. BRADFORD, Alfred S. *With Arrow, Sword, and Spear: A History of Warfare in the Ancient World.* Westport, Conn.: Praeger, 2001.

124. "Art of War" Sun Tzu; Translated from the Chinese by Lionel Giles, M.A. (1910)

125. Yeltsin draws bitter wrath of Chechens, CNN, April 22, 1996

126. "*ARMY OF GOD*" CLAIMS RESPONSIBILITY FOR *ATLANTA BOMBINGS;* Reuters News Agency, 1997 - FEB - 24; Associated Press, 1997 - FEB - 26

127. NARAL Pro-Choice America Foundation. (2006). Clinic violence and intimidation. Retrieved April 13, 2006.

128. Officials Link Atlanta Bombings and Ask for Help By KEVIN SACK Published: Tuesday, June 10, 1997

129. Anti-Abortion Extremists 'Patriots' and racists converge *By Frederick Clarkson Intelligence Report* Summer 1998 Southern Poverty Law Center

130. History Commons Timeline; Various articles sources regarding testimonies and sources concerning 911 hijackers fighting or plans to fight for Chechen mujahideen; .[Observer, 9/23/01 , ABC News, 1/9/02]

131. Reuters has reported: "Western diplomats play down any Chechen involvement by al-Qaeda." [Reuters, 10/24/02]

132. Yasenev's allegations that "Surikov has contacts with F. Ermarth, " Surikov responded: "I am personally acquainted with Mr. Ermarth as political scientist since 1996. It's well known by many people and we never hid this fact." Email between Anton Surikov and Oleg Grechenevsky 09/17/05 http://www.mail-archive.com/cia-drugs@yahoogroups.com/msg01967.html Original source; Cf. *Argumenty i Facty*, 9/15/99, http://www.aif.ru/oldsite/986/art010.html.
133. Al - Qaeda kingpin: I trained 9/11 hijackers Chris Gourlay and Jonathan Calvert The Sunday Times November 25, 2007
134. Justice Department Probe Foiled By Shane Harris and Murray Waas, *National Journal* Thursday, May 25, 2006
135. http://www.autonomy.com/content/News/Releases/2007/0625a.en.html
136. http://www.globalcrossing.com/news/2005/october/10.aspx
137. "Ring, Possible Links with Taliban," *Le Soir* [Brussels], 9 February 2002. <http://www.nisat.org>
138. Judy Pasternak and Stephen Braun, "Following the Trail of Arms to Al-Qaida," *Los Angeles Times*, 21 January 2002. <http://www.nisat.org>
139. Halliburton cases of Corruption, http://www.halliburtonwatch.org/about_hal/about.html
140. Project on Government Oversight Federal Contract Misconduct Database http://www.contractormisconduct.org/
141. Arms and the Man By PETER LANDESMAN Published: Sunday, August 17, 2003 New York Times Magazine
142. Dick Cheney Rules June 3, 2007 EDITORIAL New York Times
143. A GLOBAL OVERVIEW OF NARCOTICS-FUNDED TERRORIST AND OTHER EXTREMIST GROUPS; *A Report Prepared by the Federal Research Division, Library of Congress under an Interagency Agreement with the Department of Defense May 2002* Researchers: LaVerle Berry, Glenn E. Curtis, Rex A. Hudson and Nina A. K. Project Manager: Rex A. Hudson
144. Ibid
145. Profiles; Douglas Feith and Richard Perle. Rightweb.org
146. Letter to President Clinton regarding support for Kosovo, Project for New American Century. http://www.newamericancentury.org/kosovomilosevicsep98.htm
147. "Storm in Moscow": A Plan of the Yeltsin "Family" to Destabilize Russia John B. Dunlop The Hoover Institution

October 8, 2004 and The Global Drug Meta-Group: Drugs, Managed Violence, and the Russian 9/11 By Peter Dale Scott

148. "Blowing up Russian" by Alexander Litvinenko and Vladimir Feltshinsky 2006 (Following the books second edition released 2006, p 65. Litvinenko was exposed to polonium a highly radioactive material. Litvinenko died but a criminal investigation is still current alleging that Litvinenko was deliberately poisoned by FSB agents or contract assassins.)

149. "Effective half-life of polonium in the human" http://www.osti.gov/energycitations/product.biblio.jsp?osti_id=71 62390. Retrieved 2009-15-08

150. "Polonium Poisoning". http://nuclearweaponarchive.org/News/PoloniumPoison.html. Retrieved 2009-15-08.

151. "Litvinenko, Nuclear Arms Trafficking and Chechens" Wayne Madsen Report, Wayne Madsen, 2007.

152. Litvinenko 'smuggled nuclear material' By Cahal Milmo, Peter Popham and Jason Bennetto The Independent *Wednesday, 29 November 2006*

153. John B. Dunlop, "Storm in Moscow": A Plan of the Yeltsin "Family" to Destabilize Russia; Original story of the Meeting at Khashoggi's villa in Southern France was printed by Versiya 1999. Other versions with separate sources printed by Le Monde and Stringer have been documented and reviewed in The Global Drug Meta-Group: Drugs, Managed Violence, and the Russian 9/11 By Peter Dale Scott. The meeting was also discussed in Alexander Litvinenko's book "Blowing Up Russia."

154. Email between Anton Surikov and Oleg Grechenevsky 09/17/05 http://www.mail-archive.com/cia-drugs@yahoogroups.com/msg01967.html original source from Cf. *Argumenty i Facty*, 9/15/99, http://www.aif.ru/oldsite/986/art010.html.

155. Interview, http://www.pravda.info/region/3601.html, discussed below. Cf. Letter of Anton Surikov to Oleg Grechenevsky,

156. The article "Rossiyu zhdet oranzhevaya revolytsiya," *compormat.ru*, 17 December 2004 reports that Davidovich lives in Munich and enjoys both German and Venezuelan citizenship. He is also said to be personally acquainted with international arms dealer Khashoggi.

157. Richard Sakwa, ed (2005). "Robert Bruce Ware: Mythology and Political Failure in Chechnya". *Chechnya: From Past to Future*. Anthem Press. pp. 79-115
158. "September 11, 2001; How much the French knew." Le Monde (Paris) 15 April, 2007
159. Findlaw US vs Zacarious Moussaoui Defense Exhibits
160. How the Moussaoui Case Crumbled By Viveca Novak In WASHINGTON Sunday, Oct. 19, 2003 Time
161. CIA's Harsh Interrogation Techniques Described: Sources Say Agency's Tactics Lead to Questionable Confessions, Sometimes to Death, *ABC News*, November 18, 2005
162. Khalid Sheikh Mohammed's '31 plots', *BBC*, March 15, 2007
163. Ibid
164. La Repubblica
165. Ibid
166. French Hijack Warning by Craig Murray April 19, 2007
167. Patterns of Global terrorism, United States Department of State 2007
168. Ibid
169. Le Monde, Paris, 4/15/2007
170. Coleen Rowley's Memo to FBI Director Robert Mueller, Time, May 21, 2002, http://www.time.com/time/covers/1101020603/memo.html
171. Ashcroft, 9/11, and Government as Victim by James Bovard The Future of Freedom Foundation; quoting 911 commission
172. Federal Bureau of Investigation memo on the Chechens and Ibn al Khattab, 4/2001 US v Zacarious defense exhibit 792
173. London Legal Attaché memo, Moussaoui's connections with Chechens in London. US v Zacarious defense exhibit
174. Shireen T. Hunter, *Islam in Russia: The Politics of Identity and Security* (Armonk, NY: M.E. Sharpe, 2004)
175. Ashcroft, 9/11, and Government as Victim by James Bovard; *author of* The Bush Betrayal *and* Terrorism & Tyranny: Trampling Freedom, Justice, and Peace to Rid the World of Evil *serves as a policy advisor for The Future of Freedom Foundation* quoting the 911 commission report.
176. FBI Special Agent Greg Jones Memo to FBIHQ, U.S v Zacarious Moussaoui defense exhibit 349
177. Judicial Watch FOIA request of Defense Intelligence agency 1998 declassified report released in 2004.

178. "Chechen Mujahidin training at Al Qaida camps in Afghanistan" UN & Conflict Monitor United Nations Issue 9, Autumn 2000

179. Leaving so soon? Geraldine Sealey Salon.com (accessed April 20, 2009)

180. The BCCI Affair; A Report to the Committee on Foreign Relations United States Senate by Senator John Kerry and Senator Hank Brown December 1992 102d Congress 2d Session Senate Print 102-140

181. "The United States of oil"; No administration has ever been more in bed with the energy industry -- but does that mean Big Oil is calling Bush's shots? By Damien Cave, Salon.com (accessed April 20, 2009)

182. CIA videos reveal the missed chances to kill Bin Laden Wrangles stopped arming of plane Yosri Fouda and Nick Fielding The Sunday Times September 4, 2005

183. USA V. Enaam M. Arnaout, 10/6/2003, pp.24-25/

184. J. Millard Burr and Robert O. Collins, Alms for Jihad: Charity and Terrorism in the Islamic World (Cambridge: Cambridge University Press, 2006) pp. 45-46.

185. Spreading Saudi Fundamentalism in U.S. Network of Wahhabi Mosques, Schools, Web Sites Probed by FBI By Susan Schmidt Washington Post Staff Writer Thursday, October 2, 2003; Page A01

186. Plane Carried 13 Bin Ladens Manifest of Sept. 19, 2001, Flight From U.S. Is Released *By Dana Milbank* Washington Post Staff Writer Thursday, July 22, 2004; Page A07

187. Press Release of Senator Lautenberg, Lautenberg, and Schumer: Why Was a Charter Plane Also Rented by White House Used to Fly Bin Laden Family Out of USA After 9/11? Friday, July 23, 2004

188. "The president ought to be ashamed"; Former Sen. Max Cleland blasts Bush's "Nixonian" stonewalling of the 9/11 commission, his "lies" about Iraq, and his flight-suit photo op on the USS Lincoln after "hiding out" during Vietnam. By Eric Boehlert http://dir.salon.com/story/news/feature/2003/11/21/cleland/index.html

189. Bush and Blair made secret pact for Iraq war; Decision came nine days after 9/11 Ex-ambassador reveals discussion David Rose The Observer, Sunday 4 April 2004 12.20 BST

190. Sibel Edmonds' State Secrets Privilege Gallery on website JUST A CITIZEN http://justacitizen.com/

191. False claims of Saddam ties to al Qaida- Seymour M. Hersh, "The Stovepipe," *New Yorker*, October 27, 2003, http://www.newyorker.com/archive/2003/10/27/031027fa_fact?printable=true

192. *Office of Special Plans* - Right Web Profile IRC-Political Research Associates; www.rightweb.irc-online.org/

193. Blair's just a Bush baby; The US President may like to have Tony by his side, but it's crystal-clear that he isn't listening; plus Sir Robin Auld's White Paper could be revived Nick Cohen, The Observer, Sunday 10 March 2002 03.12 GMT

194. "Norwegian Jihad" Produced by ABC Australia Distributed by Journeyman Pictures, November 26, 2007

195. Saudis flown Out of US 9/13/01 Under FBI Supervision http://www.saintpetersburgtimes.com/2004/06/09/Tampabay/TIA_now_verifies_flig.shtml

196. Allegations of Iraqi intelligence providing al Qaida in Biological, Chemical and Radiological training Senate Report on Prewar Intelligence of Iraq, page 329 http://intelligence.senate.gov/phaseiiaccuracy.pdf

197. "Norwegian intelligence knew of CIA agents". Aftenposten. 2006-08-01. http://www.aftenposten.no/nyheter/iriks/article1406229.ece. Retrieved on 2009-04-20. translation, mirror

198. Sourcewatch, Office of Special Council

199. "Extraordinary rendition" -The hunt for "Mister Bob" and the 18 bastards By: Fausto Giudice 11/18/05 Translated from French by Ragnar B. Johannessen

200. Suspect CIA agents were in Norway by Jonathan Tisdall Aftenposten. http://www.aftenposten.no/english/local/article1397884.ece?service=print

201. Italian spies 'faked documents' on Saddam nuclear purchase By Nicholas Rufford The Sunday Times August 1, 2004

202. American Committee for Peace in Chechnya: Members http://www.peaceinchechnya.org/about_members.htm

203. Walsh, LE (1993-08-04), *Final Report of the Independent Counsel for Iran/Contra Matters; volume I: "Investigations and Prosecution"*, Washington, D.C.

204. Bob, 007 senza limiti. Chi lo ha coperto? Guido Olimpio 24 giugno 2005 *Corriere della Sera*

205. Ibid

206. "How one man insinuated himself into poisoning case"
     International Herald Tribune, 9 January 2007.
207. Il falso dossier di Scaramella - "Così la Russia manipola Prodi",
     La Repubblica, 11 January 2007
208. Ibid
209. National Research Council, Protecting Individual Privacy in the
     Struggle Against Terrorists: A Framework for Program
     Assessment, Washington DC: National Academies Press, 2008.
210. Marc Grossman, Vice Chairman of Cohen Group
     http://www.cohengroup.net/about/teammember.cfm?id=5
211. Grossman, Traavik Meet in Oslo on NATO Enlargement,
     Summit, April 19, 2002; Norwegian Ministry of Foreign Affairs
     Oslo, Norway April 19, 2002
     http://italy.usembassy.gov/viewer/article.asp?article=/file2002_0
     4/alia/A2042304.htm
212. Møte med fyrsten Richard Perle snakker med lav, behagelig
     stemme. Men det han sier, er egnet til å skremme. By HALVOR
     ELVIK Published Friday 27 February, 2004 Dagbladet News

www.ingramcontent.com/pod-product-compliance
Lightning Source LLC
Chambersburg PA
CBHW050114280326
41933CB00010B/1089